ALL THE

Glorious

NAMES

ALL THE

Glorious

NAMES

A 40-Day
Experience with God

MARY FOXWELL LOEKS

W PUBLISHING GROUP

AN IMPRINT OF THOMAS NELSON

Published in Nashville, Tennessee, by W Publishing, an imprint of Thomas Nelson.

Journaling prompts written by Ami McConnell.

Unless otherwise noted, Scripture quotations are taken from The Holy Bible, *New International Version*®. Copyright © 1973, 1978, 1984 by Biblica, Inc.® Used by permission. All rights reserved. The "NIV" and "New International Version" are trademarks registered in the United States Patent and Trademark Office by Biblica, Inc.®

Scripture quotations marked KJV are from the King James Version. Public domain.

Scripture quotations marked RSV are from the Revised Standard Version of the Bible. Copyright 1946, 1952, and 1971, National Council of the Churches of Christ in the United States of America. Used by permission. All rights reserved.

Scripture quotations marked MLB are from *The Modern Language Bible—The New Berkeley Version in Modern English,* Revised Version (MLB). © 1945, 1959, 1969 by Hendrickson Publishers, Inc.

Scripture quotations marked TNIV are from the Holy Bible, Today's New International® Version TNIV®. Copyright 2001, 2005 by International Bible Society®. Used by permission of International Bible Society®. All rights reserved worldwide. "TNIV" and "Today's New International Version" are trademarks registered in the United States Patent and Trademark Office by International Bible Society®.

Scripture quotations marked THE MESSAGE are from *The Message.* Copyright © by Eugene H. Peterson 1993, 1994, 1995, 1996, 2000, 2001, 2002. Used by permission of Tyndale House Publishers, Inc.

ISBN 978-0-7852-3765-5

Printed in India

20 21 22 23 24 REP 10 9 8 7 6 5 4 3 2 1

To John,
who suggested the idea for this book

CONTENTS

Join All the Glorious Names

Isaac Watts

John Darwall

Words: Isaac Watts, 1707
Music: William Croft, 1708
Alternate Tune: John Darwall, 1770

PREFACE

*P*erhaps you received this book as a gift. Each of the names of God is a gift to us, lighting up a facet of who God is, and lighting it up as clearly as when that name was first given us in Scripture. This is a book of invitations to worship. I invite you to think of your written responses as part of that worship. Each meditation is an attempt to attribute worth to our God by naming one of God's names. They are designed to be used in private worship, but they could also be used by those who wish to lead a group in a brief time of focusing on God, and who God is.

As I have reread the words I typed on my manual typewriter over three decades ago, I have been struck by the fact that, while much in my life and in our world has changed, our God has not changed! I am truly honored by the decision of HarperCollins to republish these meditations.

As I have studied these names, I have been impressed with how many pairs of them stand in stark contrast to each other! God is the Lord and the Servant. God is the Lamb and the Lion and the Lioness. God is the Shepherd and the Lamb. The Alpha and the Omega, the Almighty and the Abba. The minute we have the audacity to think we understand, God brings to mind another name, equally true but which seems to shatter the mold into which we have just tried to cram our very great God.

Looking at these contrasting pairs of names is like seeing only the "legs" of a giant parabola! We know they meet and are one, even if we don't see quite how.

I pray these meditations will serve as aperitifs to whet your appetite for your own further reflection and study. I invite you to name the names of our God with me, and as you do so, be full of wonder that our great God has said, "I have called *you* by name, you are mine" (Isaiah 43:1 RSV, emphasis added).

MARY FOXWELL LOEKS

ALPHA

Scripture: Genesis 1:1–2; John 1:1–14

In the beginning was the Word, and the Word was with God, and the Word was God. He was with God in the beginning. (John 1:1–2)

I am the **Alpha** . . . , the First . . . , the Beginning. (Rev. 22:13)

*T*ime had a beginning. Creation had a beginning. We had a beginning. Civilizations have a beginning. Books have a beginning. All of the endeavors we would undertake have their beginning.

But God? God has no beginning. Before any other beginning began, God was. "Before Abraham was born, I am!" declared Jesus (John 8:58). Why, then, would the eternal God have named himself Alpha, the first letter of the Greek alphabet, the beginning? It must have been because God is the great Beginner of all other beginnings! "Through him all things were made; without him nothing was made that has been made" (John 1:3).

> Christ, to thee, with God the Father,
> And, O Holy Ghost, to thee,
> Hymn and chant and high thanksgiving,
> And unwearied praises be:
> Honor, glory, and dominion,
> And eternal victory,
> Evermore and evermore.
>
> —AURELIUS CLEMENS PRUDENTIUS (348–c. 410)

Alpha God, we lay before you that which we will attempt to begin this day. We acknowledge that without you, all our attempts at beginnings are in vain. We can't see what will result from that which we now begin. Apprehension is mixed with our enthusiasm. We place it before you, Alpha God, knowing that you see not just the beginning but the whole.

We worship you; we build our lives upon you, our Alpha God, who is truly without beginning.

What new thing is God beginning in your life? Maybe it's something physical or even emotional or spiritual. How might you trust God with that new thing? Write about it below.

THE DOOR

Scripture: Exodus 12:7; John 10:1–10

I am **the door**. Whoever comes in through Me shall be saved; they will go in and out and find pasture. (John 10:9 MLB)

*T*hey were very ordinary doors, set in very ordinary houses. Their uniqueness lay only in the fact that their frames had been freshly painted with lamb's blood.

These doors closed out the cold night air and the turmoil and pain of the outside world. The angel of death was engaged in a terrible mission that night. Relentlessly, one by one, he summoned the firstborn in all the other houses. But he would not violate the closed doors framed in lamb's blood. Within these doors were peace and a quiet expectancy that could not be understood by those outside.

The next morning, many walked out through those same blood-framed doors. They left behind their slavery. The open door led them to opportunity and freedom.

Jesus Christ is the Door those doors of long ago were pointing toward. The frame is painted with his blood.

Jesus Christ is the Door that closes out that which would destroy us, providing us peace and safety as we take refuge behind him.

Jesus Christ is the Door that opens up to us opportunity, freedom, and "life . . . to the full" (John 10:10).

Today we claim his protection. We claim the abundant life to which he would lead us. And we may claim the Lamb's blood on his doorframe.

We love you, Lord Jesus, our Door. It is through you we have gained our entrance. Now enter us, we pray, and fill us with yourself this day.

What might be keeping you from entering through Jesus the Door today? Write about whatever it is here, handing it over into his faithful care.

JESUS

Scripture: Matthew 1:18–24; Revelation 22:20–21

She will give birth to a son, and you are to give him the name Jesus, because he will save his people from their sins. (Matt. 1:21)

Above his head they placed the written charge against him: THIS IS JESUS, THE KING OF THE JEWS. (Matt. 27:37)

Therefore God exalted him to the highest place and gave him the name that is above every name, that at the name of Jesus every knee should bow, in heaven and on earth and under the earth, and every tongue confess that Jesus Christ is Lord, to the glory of God the Father. (Phil. 2:9–11)

By faith in the name of Jesus, this man whom you see and know was made strong. It is Jesus' name and the faith that comes through him that has given this complete healing to him, as you can all see. (Acts 3:16)

He who testifies to these things says, "Yes, I am coming soon." Amen. Come, Lord Jesus. The grace of the Lord Jesus be with God's people. Amen. (Rev. 22:20–21)

*M*any names, when traced to their origin, describe the job or occupation of the one so named: Smith, Taylor (tailor), Baker, Butler, Fisher, Carpenter. The Gospel writer Matthew records a dream in which Joseph was told to name the son his wife-to-be, Mary, would bear Jesus, because of the job he would do. He would save his people from their sin. Jesus is the Savior.

Sin sometimes comes in a gilded wrapping, but when viewed for what it is, it is never a pretty subject. Sin is ugly. It is a slap in the face of God. It cannot go unpunished.

Greek and Roman mythology is full of tales of how the gods punished mortals for various sins committed against them.

Arachne was a young Greek girl whose pride was her downfall. She thought she could weave more skillfully than the goddess Athena and challenged the goddess to a competition. As a punishment, Arachne and her descendants were changed forever into the form of spiders.

Sisyphus had the audacity to trick the gods into giving him something he wanted. For his punishment, he was made to push a huge boulder up a steep hill. Every time it almost reached the top, it would slip from his hands and roll back down, and he was made to roll it back up again, and again, and again—eternally.

Tantalus murdered his son in a misguided attempt to make an offering to the gods. The gods punished him by making him stand forever in water up to his neck. But he was never able to quench his thirst, for whenever he bent to drink, the water receded. Above his head hung branches loaded with fruit, but whenever he tried to pick one, the branch bent out of his reach.

You and I have sinned. We deserve eternal punishment, just as did the sinful humans depicted in the Greek myths. But unlike the gods, which are creations of human imagination, the real

God truly loves the people he made, even though they are sinful. So Jesus came.

Jesus himself wore our pride to the cross. Unlike Arachne, we won't need to wear its consequences throughout eternity.

Jesus himself carried the huge boulder of our sin to the cross—and rolled it away forever.

Jesus freed us from our sin by his death on the cross and put living water eternally within our reach.

There is power in the name of Jesus. It is the power to forgive sins and to change lives. The blind man, Bartimaeus, received his sight when he called on the name of Jesus (Mark 10:46–52). Peter and John invoked the power of the name of Jesus, and a lame man began to walk and leap and praise God (Acts 3:1–16). A meeting with the Jesus he had been persecuting completely turned around the life of the man Saul of Tarsus. And there will come a day when every knee in heaven, on earth, and under the earth will bow, acknowledging at last that Jesus Christ is Lord.

> I lay my sins on Jesus, the spotless Lamb of God;
> He bears them all, and frees us from the accursed load:
> I bring my guilt to Jesus, to wash my crimson stains
> White in his blood most precious, 'till not a spot remains.
> —HORATIUS BONAR, 1843

It is at your name that we bow today, Lord Jesus, and our tongues confess you as Lord. To God be all glory!

It's such a gift to be able to call on the name of Jesus for matters large and small. Try whispering the name of Jesus and note how the atmosphere in the room changes. Write about it here.

4

THE GOD
WHO SEES ME

Scripture: Genesis 16; 21:8–20

She gave this name to the LORD who spoke to her:
"You are the God who sees me," for she said, "I have
now seen the One who sees me." (Gen. 16:13)

*D*uring the construction of the National Cathedral in Washington, D.C., a visitor stopped to watch an elderly stone carver working painstakingly at his craft. The visitor noted that when this particular piece of carving was put in place, it would be next to the wall, where no one could see it.

"Why are you working so hard on something no one will ever see?" asked the amazed onlooker.

"God will see it," replied the carver.

Sometimes it is a little unsettling to realize that ours is a God who is all-seeing! We'd rather put our mistakes and blemishes in the shadows, in a corner, against a wall—anything to get them out of sight. At times we succeed in hiding that which we wish to hide from other people, but we never can hide it from God's penetrating, purifying gaze:

> The eyes of the LORD are everywhere,
> keeping watch on the wicked and the good.
>
> (PROV. 15:3)

But there are other times when, like Hagar, we marvel with gratitude at the God who sees. The problems we encounter that no one else seems to understand—God sees.

> He will not let your foot slip—
> he who watches over you will not slumber;
> indeed, he who watches over Israel
> will neither slumber nor sleep.
> The LORD watches over you—
> the LORD is your shade at your right hand;
> the sun will not harm you by day,
> nor the moon by night,

The LORD will keep you from all harm—
> he will watch over your life;

The LORD will watch over your coming and going
> both now and forevermore.

(Ps. 121:3–8)

Our Seeing God penetrates and purges the dark corners of our sinfulness.

Our Seeing God protects and preserves us from danger.

Our Seeing God feels our private pain along with us.

Seeing God, we praise your name! Today we trust you with the thoughts of our hearts and the works of our hands which are unseen by others. Today we trust you with the future we cannot see, grateful that you will see us into it and through it.

We sometimes fool ourselves into thinking God is occupied by other, more important matters. What worries have you let fool you into thinking God doesn't see? Are there dark corners you wish God wouldn't see? Write about them and hand them over to God here.

5

LORD

Scripture: Psalm 8; Isaiah 40:3–5

O LORD, our Lord, how majestic is your name in all the earth! (Ps. 8:1)

And the glory of the LORD will be revealed, and all mankind together will see it. For the mouth of the LORD has spoken. (Isa. 40:5)

On his robe and on his thigh he has this name written: . . . LORD OF LORDS. (Rev. 19:16)

The title *lord* has lost some of its impact in our egalitarian culture. In feudal society, a lord was a man of high rank, perhaps even a king. He might have been the proprietor of a manor or a man who had mastery in a given field. The relationship of servants to their lord was a formal, respectful one. The title *lord* demanded unquestioning obedience from the servant.

The disciple Peter's outburst, "Surely not, Lord! . . . I have never eaten anything impure or unclean" (Acts 10:14), was a contradiction in terms. To say "surely not" in response to his Lord's invitation was to deny lordship. That what Peter was asked to do ran counter to the customs and traditions with which he had been brought up was not a consideration.

But before we are too hard on Peter, we need to consider our own responses:

"But, Lord . . ."
"Not me, Lord . . ."
"No, Lord."
"Lord, why?"

Sometimes our outbursts are spoken, sometimes not. Our Lord has every right to say to his disciples and to us, "Why do you call me, 'Lord, Lord,' and do not do what I say?" (Luke 6:46).

The problem with feudal lords was that they were not all-knowing, so they sometimes made unwise demands. Some did not truly love their servants, so they misused the power of their lordship.

We need not fear that kind of abuse of power. The One we call Lord loved us enough to give his own life for us. He is all-knowing and all-wise. The commands he gives us spring from that love and that wisdom and demand our obedience. One servant wrote of this Lord:

Were the whole realm of nature mine,
That were a present far too small;
Love so amazing, so divine,
Demands my soul, my life, my all.

—ISAAC WATTS, 1709

Lord of Lords, today we bow before you, acknowledging your greatness and goodness. Accept now our worship, we pray.

Acknowledging someone's power over us can make us feel anxious and even fearful. Is trusting Jesus as our ultimate authority different? How? Write about that difference here.

6

SERVANT

Scripture: John 13:1–17; Philippians 2:1–11; Isaiah 42:1

Here is my servant, whom I uphold, my chosen one in whom I delight; I will put my Spirit on him and he will bring justice to the nations. (Isa. 42:1; cf. Matt 12:18)

Jesus knew that the Father had put all things under his power, and that he had come from God and was returning to God; so he got up from the meal, took off his outer clothing, and wrapped a towel around his waist. After that, he poured water into a basin and began to wash his disciples' feet, drying them with the towel that was wrapped around him. (John 13:3–5)

Your attitude should be the same as that of Christ Jesus: Who, being in very nature God, did not consider equality with God something to be grasped, but made himself nothing, taking the very nature of a servant, being made in human likeness. (Phil. 2:5–7)

*T*he dinner guests all arrived on foot. Open sandals were all that protected their feet from the dusty roads. Customarily, a servant from the host's household would have met them at the door and washed and dried their feet. That nicety had been overlooked this particular night. It was to a borrowed room that this group had come to observe the Passover Feast. One of the men seated at the table slipped from his place, stripped down to the short tunic, which was all a servant would have worn, and wrapped a towel about himself. He went around the group without a word, kneeling at the feet of each of the men present, and washed and dried them. Until he reached the place of the man called Peter. Undoubtedly all of the men realized the incongruity of the situation—they probably all felt a little sheepish. Here was the man they called Lord and Teacher performing a most menial task for them! But their sheepishness had rendered them speechless. Except for Peter.

"Not my feet!" Peter protested.

But Jesus was insistent. "Unless I wash you, you have no part with me" (John 13:8).

Who was this guest-turned-servant? He was truly God. But he did not grasp his God-ness. He set it aside and submitted to servanthood.

His was not a conditional submission: I'll submit to you if you submit to me; or I'll serve you if you'll give me lots of sympathy for doing this miserable job; or I'll do it in exchange for a generous supply of credit, attention, and pats on the back.

Most of us don't understand servanthood very well. Jesus laid aside his God-ness to help us understand. Being a servant means considering others better than oneself. It means looking out for the other person's interests and needs first. Being a servant means being obedient. It means attributing all credit and honor to the one served. To truly serve takes the truest sort of nobility.

The One whose name is above every name knelt and washed dirty feet to set an example for us.

> May the mind of Christ my Savior
> Live in me from day to day
> By His love and power controlling
> All I do and say.

> May His beauty rest upon me
> As I seek the lost to win.
> And may they forget the channel
> Seeing only Him.[1]

—KATE B. WILKINSON (1859–1928)

Servant Lord, You have shown us how to serve. Now open our eyes to the feet that need washing, the wounds that need binding, and the burdens that need lifting this day. May we wash, bind, and lift as though they were your feet, your wounds, and your burdens.

Jesus washed the feet of the disciples to demonstrate his love. Write the names of three people you love, then write how you might show them love through service this week. List a specific way you might serve each one, but be ready to serve however God prompts you in the moment.

7

THE WAY

Scripture: John 14:1–6; Hebrews 10:19–25; Psalm 1

The blood of Jesus, . . . a new and living way opened for us. (Heb. 10:19–20)

I am the way . . . No one comes to the Father except through me. (John 14:6)

*T*he lone mountain climber, partway up Mount Fuji, reached a fork in the trail. One of the trails was marked by a sign, its message painted boldly and clearly. This was the way the climber chose to follow. The mountain climber was a scholar, conversant in a number of classical and modern languages. But he didn't know Japanese and thus couldn't read the message on that boldly painted sign. The message read: "Danger! This way should be attempted only by the most skilled and experienced climbers." Having taken the wrong way, this climber fell and lost his life.

Signs clutter our streets and highways. Sometimes they amuse us; sometimes they disgust us; sometimes they provide useful information. The intent of the one who places a sign is that we will pursue a certain prescribed course of action or follow in a certain way.

Because of sin, we have lost our way. We are without direction or purpose and have no hope of finding reconciliation with the Father. The bridge is out. There is no crossing the deep chasm created by sin.

But Jesus, like a bold signpost, declares authoritatively, "I am the way . . . No one comes to the Father except through me." Then Jesus literally, physically became the Way. His death on our behalf provided the bridge to cross the chasm. It made possible our reconciliation with the Father.

There are those who resent the exclusiveness Jesus implies: "No one comes . . . except through me." "God isn't being fair," they say. "There must be another way for those who mean well and try hard but haven't encountered the Way." If that were true, if there had been any other way, then the Father God's act of sending his dearly beloved Son to shoulder the world's sin as he died on the cross was the most hideously absurd act ever committed.

Unlike the sign on Mount Fuji, Jesus' message, "I am the Way," is clear and can be read by all. But the consequence of taking a wrong way, even with the best of intentions, is certain death.

The Way is not always smoothly paved. Following the Way is not always easy. It is not always fun. It does not always follow the most scenic route. Sometimes our feet will hurt; sometimes we will be bone-tired. Sometimes we will be lonely. At other times, the rudeness of other travelers along the way will irritate us. Sometimes we will wish we could turn back; we may even wonder at times if we have made a mistake.

But the Way is sure and leads to a sure end—eternal life through Jesus Christ, our Lord.

Jesus, our Way, we are hopelessly, helplessly lost without you. Give us direction today for the next step you would have us take.

Recall a specific time when you felt literally lost. Write below about how that felt. When you found your way again, how did that feel? Be reminded today that we have ultimate access to The Way: Jesus Christ.

8

THE TRUTH

Scripture: Psalm 25:4–5, 8–9; John 8:31–32

Jesus answered, "I am . . . the truth . . . No one comes to the Father except through me." (John 14:6)

Jesus said, "If you hold to my teaching, you are really my disciples. Then you will know the truth, and the truth will set you free." (John 8:31–32)

*G*oaded by his fickle subjects, Pontius Pilate allowed the Truth to slip through his fingers, unnamed and unclaimed. He asked the right question, but he would not allow himself to see that the answer stood right before him.

Acknowledging the Truth would not have been politically expedient for Pontius Pilate. Indeed, pursuing truth can be costly, inconvenient, uncomfortable, and even dangerous. Many of us know people who have lost friends, jobs, material things, or their lives because they pursued truth.

But Pilate was mistaken if he really thought he could wash his hands of his responsibility to deal with the Truth (Matt. 27:24). Exposure to the Truth demands a response. For the One who said, "I am . . . the truth" went on to say, "No one comes to the Father except through me." By choosing the politically expedient way, Pilate lost his opportunity to find the Way and the Truth.

Truth is a searching spotlight, leaving no shadows in which to hide for those intent on pursuing evil. But for those seeking to follow God, this same spotlight is a welcome revealer of the obstacles over which they might otherwise have stumbled.

For us who would belong to God, following the Truth is not optional. The apostle Paul urges us to think on "whatsoever things are true" (Phil. 4:8 KJV). But like pure water and pure air around us, pure truth is hard to come by. The clarity of truth may be shadowed by unbelief, impure motives, and careless inattention. The impact of truth without love is like that of surgery on one whose body is incapable of healing. The impact of truth without wisdom is like that of light shining on the path of a blind person.

The beauty of Jesus, our Truth, is that he is the God of love as well as the God of wisdom. Jesus is God's true expression of himself.

Jesus Christ, our Truth, we worship you! Our falseness makes us squirm, but we know that we dare not, cannot hide. We confess that we have sinned. Realign us today next to the yardstick of your truth.

Sometimes the truth is a relief and sometimes it makes us squirm—especially when truth requires us to make a change. Take a moment to listen. What does Truth whisper to you today? Write about it here.

9

THE LIFE

Scripture: John 11:1–44

I am . . . the life. No one comes to the Father except through me. (John 14:6)

Jesus said to her, "I am the resurrection and the life. Anyone who believes in me will live, even though they die; and whoever lives by believing in me will never die." (John 11:25–26 TNIV)

*I*n the nine long months of waiting for a child to be born, we can see the ever-expanding belly—an indication of the new little life within it. We can feel, even sometimes see the baby's movements—surely this one will be a gymnast! And with the technology now available, we can hear our baby's heartbeat, watch movements in utero, know the gender, and learn much about this child for whom we wait. And wait.

Finally the day arrives, the newborn emerges, and the cord is clamped. Several seconds pass, each seeming like an eternity. Then we hear it, the first wail of this newborn baby! This is the cry that declares for all to hear, "I am breathing on my own. I am receiving the life you have hoped for, prayed for, and labored for." The gift of life demands a response.

The commencement of eternal life is also signaled by a birth, sometimes referred to as the second birth. Jesus told Nicodemus that "unless one is born anew, he cannot see the kingdom of God" (John 3:3 RSV). God himself, in the person of Jesus, has experienced indescribably excruciating labor to make our new birth possible. Others may have hoped and prayed for it to happen. Perhaps it is inevitable, but there must indeed come a time of affirmation, the baby's first wail: "Yes, I am receiving this life. Yes, I acknowledge the implications. I realize, as did the apostle Paul, that 'I have been crucified with Christ and I no longer live, but Christ lives in me'" (Gal. 2:20).

Naming Jesus Life gets at the very essence of what Christianity is all about. But in order to be Life for us, he first had to be our death. And because of who he was, God-man, his very real death could be followed by a very real coming alive, a resurrection.

Jesus felt pain at the death of his friend Lazarus. He wept. But the One who named himself both the Resurrection and the Life was able to lock this pain of death into that small sliver of eternity known as time.

Thou only art true Life,
To know Thee is to live
The more abundant life
That earth can never give:
O risen Lord! We live in Thee,
And Thou in us eternally.[2]

—E. Margaret Clarkson

*Jesus Christ, because you first named yourself the
Resurrection and the Life, we are able to call you by these
names today. In doing so, we strain to catch a glimpse of
what that abundant life, lived beyond time, will mean.
Live through us today.*

What image comes to mind when you consider the word "death"? What images come to mind when you consider the word "life"? Name two ways you can celebrate Life today.

10

ETERNAL GOD

Scripture: Deuteronomy 33:26–29; Romans 1:20

The eternal God is your refuge, and underneath are the everlasting arms. (Deut. 33:27)

Now to the King eternal, immortal, invisible, the only God, be honor and glory for ever and ever. Amen. (1 Tim. 1:17)

*F*ettered by time as we are, it is hard for us to imagine what the word *eternal* means. People are born and they die. We light a match to start a fire, and when the wood is consumed, it extinguishes itself. Tasks are begun and they are completed. A day begins with the sun's apparent rising and ends when the sun appears to set. We hang a new calendar on the wall when a year begins and take it down when a year ends. What is it never to have begun and never to end? Who is the eternal God? What does eternity mean, anyway?

A simple math problem brings to mind one picture of eternity: the problem is to divide three into one. Now, there is a long math problem! Infinitely, eternally long! In fact, if someone starts to work that problem today, it will never be completed, even if that person keeps working through all eternity! Our mathematicians will simply have to decide when to go on to other things. For no matter how many times the three is divided into the one, the one is never completely used up.

The eternal One who is our God has made all his resources available for us to draw on. Even when we are released from the bondage of time, we can keep drawing from the eternal One strength, grace, wisdom, and all that we need throughout all of eternity. The supply will never be exhausted.

Infinite, Eternal One! Unwittingly we limit you with our finity and shortsightedness. Help us to see more clearly what it means to draw on your infinite, eternal resources. We entrust the time you have given us today back to you, mindful that our times are truly in your hands. And you have made a way for us to share eternity with you. Receive our deep gratitude this day, Father of Eternity, Infinite, Eternal One!

In our busy lives, it can sometimes feel like there isn't enough time. Take a few deep breaths and remember that time is not a limitation for God. God is never at a loss for time. Write down two things that demand lots of your time and entrust them to Eternal God for safekeeping. He is faithful!

11

THE MORNING STAR

Scripture: John 1:4–9; 3:19–21

I, Jesus, have sent my angel to give you this testimony for the churches. I am . . . the bright Morning Star. (Rev. 22:16)

To him who overcomes and does my will to the end, I will give authority over the nations . . . I will also give him the morning star. (Rev. 2:26, 28)

I see him, but not now; I behold him, but not near. A star will come out of Jacob; a scepter will rise out of Israel. (Num. 24:17)

*W*hat is a star? Stars are not the mysteries they once were. Thanks to modern science, we can understand their composition, how far away they are, and how large they are with much more clarity than did our ancestors.

What is a star? A star is a source of light. That light comes from the burning up of its very essence. It is not reflected light, such as comes to us from the moon and planets.

Perhaps understanding these two types of light can help us to understand Jesus' two seemingly paradoxical statements, "I am the light of the world" and "you are the light of the world." Like a bright and burning ball of fire, Jesus is our source of light. As we reflect his light, we, too, can be light to our world.

To be light, a light source must spend itself. It must literally use itself up. It is difficult for us to fathom what that means for a star, because the "using up" takes place over millions or perhaps billions of years. But consider a burning candle.* Even as we watch it give light for us, we can see that the candle is being used up, spent.

How like our Lord! In order to be light for us, he literally spent himself.

> O Splendor of God's glory bright,
> From light eternal bringing light,
> Thou Light of light, light's living Spring
> True Day, all days illumining;
>
> Come, very Sun of heaven's love,
> In lasting radiance from above,
> And pour the Holy Spirit's ray
> On all we think or do today.

---

* If you are using this meditation with a group, you might like to have a candle burning while you talk.

Dawn's glory gilds the earth and skies,
Let him, our perfect Morn, arise,
The Word in God the Father one,
The Father imaged in the Son.

—AMBROSE OF MILAN (340–397)

Jesus, our bright Morning Star! Forgive us for taking for granted what it cost you to be light for us.

Jesus, our bright Morning Star! Help us this day to be clearer reflectors of your light, so that we, too, may "shine like stars in the universe as [we] hold out the word of life" (Phil. 2:15–16).

Close your eyes and take a moment to remember what it's like to glimpse a bright star on the backdrop of a dark sky. The contrast is intense! How is Jesus like a bright star in your life? Have you seen the light of Jesus today? In what way(s)?

12

ROCK

I love you, O LORD, my strength.
The LORD is my rock, my fortress and my deliverer;
    my God is my rock, in whom I take refuge.
      He is my shield and the horn of my salvation, my
        stronghold.
For who is God besides the LORD?
    And who is the Rock except our God?
The LORD lives! Praise be to my Rock!
    Exalted be God my Savior!
          (Ps. 18:1–2, 31, 46)

He lifted me out of the slimy pit,
    out of the mud and mire;
    he set my feet on a rock
    and gave me a firm place to stand.
        (Ps. 40:2)

ave you ever considered how truly desperate Jacob must have been to choose a rock for a pillow? A rock is hardly a comfortable place to sit for a long time, let alone to sleep on all night. A prolonged or abrupt encounter with a rock is not what most of us would consider comfortable—it can indeed be downright painful!

But there is a big difference between comfortable and comforting. A rock is a secure place on which to build. Unlike the house built on shifting sand, the house built on the rock withstood the ravages of rain and flood (Matt. 7:24).

A rock is a safe place on which to stand after one has been slipping and sliding about in quicksand (Ps. 40:2). A large rock is secure, fixed, and unmovable. It represents constancy and permanence, something to grab hold of when everything else about us seems to be changing.

A rock can be a shelter under which to take refuge. It can provide shade from a merciless sun or spare one from the fury of a driving rain.

An abrupt encounter with a rock cannot be ignored. We cannot pretend it isn't there, especially if the encounter has been painful. Jacob slept with a rock for a pillow. He dreamed and afterward awoke with an awareness of the presence of the Lord. He made a solemn vow as his response (Gen. 28:10–22). In the parable of the tenants (Mark 12:1–12), the visit of the owner's beloved son could not be ignored. The response of the tenants was to reject and kill the owner's son. As Jesus concluded his parable, he quoted Scripture:

> The stone the builders rejected
>> has become the capstone;
>> the Lord has done this,
>> and it is marvelous in our eyes.
>
> (MARK 12:10–11)

The same stone will be tripped over by some and used as a firm place to stand by others (Isa. 8:14; 28:16).

Jesus Christ is my Rock. He is my refuge, my foundation, my resting place, and my security in the midst of turmoil. The reality of who he is and what he has done looms large in front of me and cannot be ignored. Today my encounter with the Rock demands a response:

> *Lord, God, "may the words of my mouth and the*
> *meditation of my heart be pleasing in your sight, O* Lord,
> *my Rock and my Redeemer." (Ps. 19:14)*

Though changes in life are inevitable, the eternal
Rock is sure. Nothing changes our Rock! What
changes in your life are you dealing with? How is
God our Rock a comfort to you in the midst of such
change? Be specific if possible.

13

HOLY SPIRIT

Scripture: John 14:15–27

And the Spirit of God was hovering over the waters. (Gen. 1:2)

God is spirit, and his worshipers must worship in spirit and in truth. (John 4:24)

But the Counselor, the Holy Spirit, whom the Father will send in my [Jesus'] name, will teach you all things and will remind you of everything I have said to you. (John 14:26)

Don't you know that you yourselves are God's temple and that God's Spirit lives in you? (1 Cor. 3:16)

We do not know what we ought to pray for, but the Spirit himself intercedes for us with groans that words cannot express. And he who searches our hearts knows the mind of the Spirit, because the Spirit intercedes for the saints in accordance with God's will. (Rom. 8:26–27)

Where can I go from your Spirit? Where can I flee from your presence? If I go up to the heavens, you are there; if I make my bed in the depths, you are there. (Ps. 139:7–8)

*S*ome of us can remember attempting to make an international telephone call before the days of electronic mail. We marvel at the ease and efficiency of today's global communication. But with the best of our information technology, there are sometimes power outages and other times when our equipment fails us. Sometimes we receive no response. Sometimes we receive a busy signal or a recording inviting us to leave a name and number after the "beep."

As wonderful as today's communication systems are, they don't begin to compare with the communication system available for an earth-child with her heavenly Father.

A four-year-old girl asked, "Can God really hear everyone who is praying?"

"Yes, he can," she was told.

"Even if a lot of people all over the world are praying at once?"

"He hears them all," was the reply.

"God must wear an awfully big shirt," reflected the child, after a pause.

Even we who are older than four are full of wonder as we think about prayer. It is because God is Spirit, and not bound to a shirt of any size, that prayer is possible. Because God is Spirit, God is always there, the line is never busy, we never get a recording, and we never have to wait.

Often we don't know what to say or what to ask or even how to ask. God, the Holy Spirit, conveys the message that we would have given if we could.

Because God is Spirit, God can be simultaneously with us and with people who are dear to us but far away. We have a link to our distant loved ones that those without God, the Spirit, cannot comprehend.

Because God is Spirit, there isn't any place we can go where God is not. It would be futile to try to hide or to run away.

Because of the function of God the Spirit, this is not the person of the Godhead that many of us focus on in our prayers and thoughts of God. When we look through a clear, clean window, we don't usually think about the window. We tend to focus on, and think about, what we see through the window. The Holy Spirit is much like that window. Because the Spirit is there, we are able to see the Father and the Son. How much and how clearly would we see if the window weren't there?

> Come, O Creator Spirit blest,
> And in our hearts take up thy rest;
> Spirit of grace with heavenly aid
> Come to the souls whom thou hast made.
>
> Show us the Father, Holy One,
> Help us to know th' Eternal Son;
> Spirit Divine, for evermore
> Thee will we trust and thee adore.
>
> —ANONYMOUS, TENTH CENTURY (LATIN);
> TRANS. GEORGE RAWSON (1807–1889)

O, Holy Spirit, breath of God! You are the great Communicator and Illuminator. We worship you today.

We often struggle to articulate in prayer just what we might want or need. Remembering that the Spirit intercedes with "groans that words cannot express" can be a huge comfort. Take a moment to express gratitude for the Holy Spirit's intercession during a time when prayers were difficult for you. Today, you can depend on the Holy Spirit.

14

LIVING WATER

Scripture: John 4; Isaiah 55

Come, all you who are thirsty, come to the waters; and you who have no money, come. (Isa. 55:1)

Then Jesus declared, "He who believes in me will never be thirsty." (John 6:35)

Wash me, and I will be whiter than snow. (Ps. 51:7)

When you pass through the waters, I will be with you; and when you pass through the rivers, they will not sweep over you. (Isa. 43:2)

Jesus answered her, "If you knew the gift of God and who it is that asks you for a drink, you would have asked him and he would have given you living water." (John 4:10)

We might value water more if we had to carry it in jars from the edge of town, bearing on our shoulders all the water our household needed each day! But even we who take our abundant water supply for granted can attest to the fact that after several hours of physical exertion on a hot day, nothing quenches thirst like a glass of cold water, no matter what the soft drink advertisers would have us think.

Another luxury that not all peoples of all cultures have been able to enjoy is that of frequent bathing—the opportunity to become clean! What a gift it is to be able to wash.

How vital water is for all that grows on the earth—trees, plants, flowers, grass, fruits, vegetables, grains, and all creatures. They all would die if it were not for water.

> The rain and the snow
> come down from heaven,
> and do not return to it
> without watering the earth
> and making it bud and flourish,
> so that it yields seed for the sower and bread for the eater.
>
> (Isa. 55:10)

And consider the power of moving water. It alters and erodes riverbanks and shorelines. Sometimes the energy from falling water has been harnessed to provide electricity for entire communities.

Buoyancy—we are sometimes inclined to forget this property of water. Good swimming instructors frequently tell their students: "Swim *through* the water; don't struggle so hard to get above it. The water itself will hold you up if you let it."

Where water is abundant, people have found ways to transport themselves and their goods through it. And children of all ages have enjoyed playing in water.

Sometimes we have gone about thirsty, dirty, parched, and powerless. God has put Living Water at our disposal, but we have sat beside our empty pails, either ignorant or afraid of the implications of Living Water. We can identify with Jill, a character in one of C. S. Lewis's *Chronicles of Narnia*:

"Are you not thirsty?" said the Lion.

"I'm *dying* of thirst," said Jill.

"Then drink," said the Lion.

"May I—could I—would you mind going away while I do?" said Jill.

The Lion answered this only by a look and a very low growl . . .

"I daren't come and drink," said Jill.

"Then you will die of thirst," said the Lion.

"O dear!" said Jill, coming another step nearer. "I suppose I must go and look for another stream then."

"There is no other stream," said the Lion.[3]

Jesus, our Living Water, forgive us. We have fought and struggled, trying to hold ourselves up in our own strength. We fail to appropriate the fact that as we rest in you, our Living Water, you are with us and are holding us up. Thank you that you yourself are what we need, and all we need, to quench our souls' thirst. We are grateful for the cleansing that you alone can provide us. We are awed at the power available to us. "The LORD is become our salvation. Today with joy, we will draw water from the wells of salvation" (Isa. 12:2–3, paraphrase). Receive our thanks this day.

Remember a time when you were thirsty and were able to enjoy a drink of clean, cold water. Recall the feel of water on your skin in a creek, stream, river, lake, or ocean—or even falling rain. Offer a prayer of thanks to God for the gift of water.

15

THE GENTLE WHISPER

Scripture: 1 Kings 19:9–18; 1 Samuel 3:2–10

The LORD said, "Go out and stand on the mountain . . . for the LORD is about to pass by." . . . And after the fire came a gentle whisper. (1 Kings 19:11–12)

*E*nter: one of God's faithful servants. God has only recently used him in a mighty and powerful way. But now this servant of the Lord is feeling alone, discouraged, and afraid.

The message comes: "Go out and stand on the mountain in the presence of the LORD, for the LORD is about to pass by" (1 Kings 19:11).

What must God's servant have felt and thought? Perhaps some skepticism. Surely some amazement. What will it sound like when the mighty Yahweh, Creator of the universe—the One who had poured fire from heaven to consume the water-drenched sacrifice offered by his servant—passes by?

Act I: A great and powerful wind rages and roars, tearing mountains apart and splitting huge rocks in two. Is the Lord God in the howling of the wind?*

Act II: Rumble, rumble! The earth itself, once so firm and solid, now begins to shake and tremble. To the helpless and uncertain onlooker, even seconds seem like eternities. Is God speaking in the midst of the earth's rumbles?

Act III: Hear now a crackling, spitting fire, blazing and consuming all in its path. Is this the sound of the Lord God passing by?

Act IV: In a dramatic contrast to what has just transpired, a peaceful stillness settles over the scene. Listen! Do you hear the gentle whisper? *The Lord God is passing by!* His servant hears and is encouraged.

> *O God, our Father, sometimes the clamor with which we are surrounded all but drowns out your gentle whisper. Help us to become better listeners. We would claim the prayer of the child Samuel: "Speak, for your servant is listening" (1 Sam. 3:10).*

---

* If you are using this with a group, you can provide a few simple sound effects. (Hide objects behind the podium or in a paper grocery sack.) For rocks breaking in the wind, hit two wooden blocks together. For the earthquake, place several wooden blocks in a shoe box and shake the box from side to side. For fire, wrinkle a piece of wax paper.

55

Sometimes God speaks in ways we cannot ignore. But sometimes we need quiet to hear his gentle whisper. What "noise" threatens your ability to hear God's voice? List three things that create noise in your life. How might you create stillness to hear from him more clearly?

16

LAST ADAM

Scripture: Genesis 2:7; Genesis 3;
1 Corinthians 15:20–25, 45–47

The LORD God formed the man from the dust of the ground
and breathed into his nostrils the breath of life, and the man
became a living being. (Gen. 2:7)

For as in Adam all die, so in Christ all will be made alive.
(1 Cor. 15:22)

So it is written: "The first man Adam became a living being;"
the last Adam, a life-giving spirit. (1 Cor. 15:45)

*I*t had been an adam* who introduced sin into the world. An adam cut the chasm that separated the holy God from the creatures who were his image bearers.

So it had to be an adam, a son of Adam, who would build the bridge to cross that chasm of eternal death. And it had to be an adam who was perfect and without sin. We cannot fully comprehend what had to happen. God himself became Adam. The eternal God became a human embryo, locked inside a woman's uterus for nine months. He was born in a barn, and his first bed was a box full of animal feed.

The infant "last Adam" must surely have cried when he was hungry or wet.

As an adult, the last Adam wept when his good friend, Lazarus, died.

After one exhausting day, he fell asleep in the boat of his fishermen friends.

He was so furious that a place of worship had been desecrated and corrupted that he made a whip and literally drove away those who were responsible.

He enjoyed relaxing at the home of his friends, Mary, Martha, and Lazarus.

The devil himself tried every one of his tricks on the last Adam, attempting in vain to find a vulnerable area.

The last Adam submitted to the most humiliating of deaths—as a criminal, on a cross. He experienced something no other adam needs to experience—total separation from the Father God.

> All praise to thee, Eternal Lord,
> Clothed in a garb of flesh and blood;

---

* *Adam* is the Hebrew word for "man" and may be derived from *adamah*, the Hebrew word for "ground."

Choosing a manger for thy throne,
While worlds on worlds are thine alone.

—MARTIN LUTHER, 1524

*Accept our worship, eternal Lord, you who became for us
the last Adam.*

It can be difficult to comprehend the humanity of Jesus—to remember that he's intimately acquainted with our sufferings, our joys, and everything in between. Name three issues you wrestle with that are purely physical. When you remember that Jesus knows what it's like to feel those things, how do you feel? Write about it below.

17

REDEEMER

Scripture: Job 19:25–27; Isaiah 44:6–8

Our **Redeemer**—the LORD Almighty is his name—is the Holy One of Israel. (Isa. 47:4)

I know that my **Redeemer** lives, and that in the end he will stand upon the earth. (Job 19:25)

*T*here is a story that some of us heard as children. A young boy made for himself a beautiful little sailboat, sanding, painting, and gluing each of its parts with great care. It became his favorite possession, and almost daily he went to sail it on the river near his home. One day a storm came up suddenly, the string on the boat broke, and the boat got away from him. He spent many days searching for the boat along the banks of the river, and he began to fear that he would never see it again.

Months later, his grandfather took him to town, and as they were poking around in a secondhand shop, the boy spotted a familiar-looking boat, high on one of the shelves, with a price tag attached to it.

"Let me see that boat," he cried. "I think that's the boat I made."

The shopkeeper obligingly took the boat from the shelf.

"See! These are my initials! I carved them in the bottom! This is my boat."

"I'm sorry, son. I bought that boat from the man who brought it into the shop. If you want the boat, you'll have to pay for it."

Sadly the boy left the shop. For the next few weeks he worked hard doing every odd job anyone would give him, carefully saving every penny.

At last he had the required amount of money. He went back to the shop and redeemed for himself the boat he had made.

The seeming injustice of having to pay for something that was one's own in the first place rankles a little. But that is the essence of what it means to redeem.

Christ our Creator made us and stamped us with his own image. Then we became separated from him.

Christ our Redeemer bought back the right to own us by paying a price so awful we cannot comprehend it.

I will sing of my Redeemer
And his wondrous love to me;
On the cruel cross he suffered
From the curse to set me free.

Sing, oh sing, of my Redeemer
With his blood he purchased me.
On the cross he sealed my pardon,
Paid the debt and made me free.

—Philip P. Bliss

Creator, Redeemer God, you have twice the right to own us. You hold our purchase agreement, signed in your blood. Yet some of us, fools that we are, keep trying to snatch back ownership for ourselves.

Give us just a glimpse, today, of what it cost you to redeem us. Receive our bodies as living sacrifices. Receive the words of our mouths and the thoughts of our hearts.

Our Redeemer God can take catastrophe and create a symphony. What in your life has God already redeemed? Write about it below. Then offer up an existing problem that has yet to be redeemed and ask God to do it again.

18

MERCIFUL GOD

Scripture: Exodus 25:10–22; Ephesians 2:1–5

"I am merciful," declares the LORD, "I will not be angry forever." (Jer. 3:12)

Your Father is merciful. (Luke 6:36)

God, have mercy on me, a sinner. (Luke 18:13)

But because of his great love for us, God, who is rich in mercy, made us alive with Christ even when we were dead in transgressions—it is by grace you have been saved. (Eph. 2:4–5)

I will sing of the mercies of the LORD for ever: with my mouth will I make known thy faithfulness to all generations. (Ps. 89:1 KJV)

*F*or God's mercy to hold any meaning for us, we must first begin to understand the intensity of God's holiness and the immensity of our sin. The depth of mercy is in direct relation to the gravity of the wrong.

Sometimes we think of mercy as a rug under which to scoot dirt, or as a frosting to fill and cover that section of the cake that fell. But mercy is more than the superficial covering or overlooking of a wrong. Such a notion makes a mockery of God's holiness. Mercy deals with the wrong itself.

In the book of Exodus, we have recorded for us the careful and detailed instructions God gave the Israelites for building the tabernacle. This was to be their place of worship. In the tabernacle was to be the ark of the covenant, which represented the presence of the holy God. The ark was to be a box, covered inside and out with gold. The box was to be made with two rings on each side, through which gold-covered poles were to be placed. No one, under any circumstance, was to touch the ark itself. In it were placed the tablets on which were inscribed the Ten Commandments, representing the law of God. A gold cover with two cherubim "of hammered gold" (Ex. 25:18) was placed on top of the ark. This cover has sometimes been called the mercy seat. The ark with this covering was placed behind a curtain. Only the high priest was allowed to enter that Most Holy Place—and he only once a year on the Day of Atonement. The Israelites had before them a promise that God's mercy would cover God's law, which they were unable to keep. They could partake of that mercy, but since the wrong had not yet been made right, their participation had to be from a distance.

At the moment of Jesus' death, the curtain, which for so many years had separated the ark and its mercy seat from view, was ripped from top to bottom. Justice had been done. God had paid dearly to right sin's wrongs. God's mercy could be available to all who would receive it. Now his mercy was accessible in a way it never had been before.

> Let us wonder,
>   grace and justice join,
>   and point to mercy's store;
> When through grace in Christ our trust is,
> Justice smiles and asks no more.
> He who washed us with his blood,
> Has secured our way to God.
>
> Let us praise and join the chorus
> Of the saints enthroned on high;
> Here they trusted him before us,
> Now their praises fill the sky:
> "Thou hast washed us with thy blood;
> Thou art worthy, Lamb of God!" Amen.
>
> —JOHN NEWTON, 1774

Merciful God, we confess before you that we have sinned, even this very day. You have not ignored our sin, even though we have a tendency to do so. You have not glossed over it, even though we try to do that as well. You have paid dearly that we might receive mercy instead of the justice we deserve. With gratitude we clothe ourselves in your righteousness today.

Mercy looks like a welcoming hug when what we deserve is a harsh penalty. Take a moment to bask in that embrace from God, then write a response of gratitude below.

19

LIKE AN EAGLE

Scripture: Deuteronomy 32:9–14;
Exodus 19:4; Isaiah 40:28–31

[The LORD] shielded him and cared for him; he guarded him
as the apple of his eye, **like an eagle** that stirs up its nest and
hovers over its young, that spreads its wings to catch them
and carries them on its pinions. The LORD alone led him.
(Deut. 32:10–12)

You yourselves have seen what I did to Egypt, and how I carried
you on **eagles' wings** and brought you to myself. (Ex. 19:4)

But those who hope in the LORD will renew their strength. They
will soar on wings like **eagles**. (Isa. 40:31)

*T*he eagle is one of the largest and most powerful birds in the world. Some eagles weigh as much as twelve or thirteen pounds and have a wingspan of about seven feet.

The nests of eagles are called eyries. They are built mainly of sticks and are often lined with fresh green leaves while they are being used. Once a year the female lays one or two eggs, and they are carefully tended, sometimes even by the male eagle, until they hatch in about forty days. Both parents then guard the nest and take food to their young.

At about eleven or twelve weeks, a curious thing happens. If the eaglets have not yet ventured forth on their own, the parent eagle "stirs" or rocks the nest, tipping the eaglets out! The young eaglets flap about in panic, still novices at this flying business. The parent eagle hovers watchfully, waiting for the critical moment. With wings spread wide, the eagle then swoops down underneath those babies and delivers them back to the security of the eyrie.

Ours is a God of powerful gentleness. Ours is a God whose timing is perfect. Like the parent eagle, God is sensitive to our needs. God knows when the nest has become too comfortable and needs a little stirring. God too watches carefully and, as with spread wings, catches us up, bringing us to himself. God wants us to learn from our fluttering and flapping. God wants us to leave behind our panic and to learn to wait on him. Then, with our eyes on our parent eagle, we will begin to know what it means to soar on eagle's wings!

Today we praise you, O God, for eagle's wings that keep us safe, help us soar, and bring us to yourself.

The image of God as parent is one of intimacy and
also subtle challenge. The challenge comes when we
imagine God stirring up the nest, encouraging us to
fly. In what ways might God be stirring up your nest?

20

AUTHOR AND EDITOR

Scripture: Ephesians 1:3–10; 2:10

Let us fix our eyes on Jesus, the author and [editor*] of our faith. (Heb. 12:2, paraphrase)

---

* The Greek has been translated "finisher" (KJV), "perfecter" (RSV, NIV, and RYRIE). My rendering, "editor," has much the same connotation.

*T*here isn't a human author who doesn't, or wouldn't, benefit from a good editor. The author conceives and births the idea, but a second pair of eyes sees it in a different way and with a fresh perspective.

A case can also be made for the idea that human editors—those who perfect, polish, and apply the finishing touches, those who see the work through to completion—need authors.

As our Author, Jesus Christ conceived the very idea of us before the foundation of the world. He made possible both our birth and our new birth.

But he hasn't stopped there. He has the will, the ability, and the authority to see us—his workmanship, his poem (Eph. 2:10)—through to completion. Paul tells the Philippians that he is confident that "he who began a good work in you will carry it on to completion until the day of Christ Jesus" (Phil. 1:6).

Sometimes we question or chafe at all the editing that is prescribed for us. But ours is not an Editor capable of error or capriciousness. Unlikely as it may seem at times, we will someday be all that we are meant to be: Jesus' masterpiece.

Lord Jesus, today we thank you that you who authored us have not given up on your work in progress. Remain with us, we pray, until we are complete in you, a poem that brings you praise!

Scripture reminds us that we are God's "workmanship" (or "masterpiece") created "to do good works, which God prepared in advance for us to do" (Ephesians 2:10). In what ways has God uniquely prepared you for where you are in life right now? Take a moment to thank God for his guidance and creativity.

21

THE GREAT SHEPHERD

Scripture: Psalm 23; Matthew 18:12–14;
John 10:1–8; Hebrews 13:20–21

Our Lord Jesus, that great Shepherd of the sheep . . .
(Heb. 13:20)

I am the good shepherd; I know my sheep and my sheep know
me—just as the Father knows me and I know the Father—and I
lay down my life for the sheep. (John 10:14–15)

A good shepherd, or pastor, must have a combination of almost paradoxical qualities.

We who are not shepherds tend to think of a pastoral scene as being peaceful and quiet. The picture is full of lush greens, blue sky, and a crystal-clear pool of water. No sounds more harsh than those of chirping birds can be heard. Our image of the shepherd tends to be that of a person both gentle and patient. The good shepherd thoughtfully provides the best nourishment and care possible for his sheep. He is willing to risk personal hardship and danger for them. With the picture as sketched so far, we like thinking of ourselves as sheep under the watch of such a shepherd!

But sheep are stupid creatures. Often they don't have the sense to follow the shepherd, and he must nudge or even push them from behind or alongside. Sheep are willful creatures, often straying, searching for something better, somewhere else.

The good shepherd knows each one of his sheep by name, and each is important to him. He will leave the rest of the flock to search for one that wanders off. The good shepherd persistently combs the countryside until he locates the missing sheep.

Here the pastoral picture changes. The once blue sky darkens with an approaching storm. The sheep is caught in a thorn bush at the brink of a precipice. The good shepherd has to act swiftly, forcefully. He places his shepherd's crook firmly around the neck of his sheep. Holding aside some of the thorny branches with one arm, the shepherd pulls—yes, yanks—his sheep free from the bush, bringing some of the thorns and smaller branches with it.

Having found shelter, the good shepherd has to pull out the thorns, one by one, as his sheep bleats in pain.

On the way home, the shepherd has to kill a wild animal that would otherwise have attacked. The sheep trembles and is afraid.

The good shepherd is indeed gentle and patient, a loving

provider of care and nourishment. He is also strong and able and will push or pull hard when love for his sheep dictates that he do so.

> The God of love my Shepherd is,
> And he that doth me feed:
> While He is mine and I am His,
> What can I want or need?
>
> He leads me to the tender grass
> Where I both feed and rest;
> Then to the streams that gently pass,
> In both I have the best.
>
> Or if I stray, He doth convert,
> And bring my mind in frame:
> And all this not for my desert,
> But for His holy name.
>
> —GEORGE HERBERT (BASED ON PSALM 23)

Great and Good Shepherd, we marvel that you know each of us by name and that you go out of your way to find us when we wander off. You provide for us with great care. We are grateful that you lead us, even sometimes carry us, through the dark and shadowy places. Lead us safely home, we pray.

Sheep are safest when grazing in herds, guarded by a shepherd. Consider the wayward sheep, unguarded. What happens when that sheep wanders alone? When it encounters a fierce predator or dangerous terrain, pain and suffering is the result. The good news is that we are *not* sheep without a shepherd. God promises to guide us and has already "laid down his life" for us (John 10:15). How is the Good Shepherd guiding you? What hazards has the Good Shepherd helped you avoid or successfully defeat?

22

LAMB

*Scripture: John 1:29–34; Revelation
5:12; 1 Corinthians 5:7–8*

Abraham answered, "God himself will provide the lamb for
the burnt offering, my son." (Gen. 22:8)

Tell the whole community of Israel that on the tenth day of this
month each man is to take a lamb for his family, one for each
household. (Ex. 12:3)

He was led like a lamb to the slaughter, and as a sheep before
her shearers is silent, so he did not open his mouth. (Isa. 53:7)

The next day John saw Jesus coming toward him and said,
"Look, the Lamb of God, who takes away the sin of the world!"
(John 1:29)

[You were redeemed] with the precious blood of Christ, a lamb
without blemish or defect. (1 Peter 1:19)

Then I saw a Lamb, looking as if it had been slain, standing in the center of the throne, encircled by the four living creatures and the elders. In a loud voice they sang: "Worthy is the Lamb, who was slain, to receive power and wealth and wisdom and strength and honor and glory and praise!" (Rev. 5:6, 12)

They have washed their robes and made them white in the blood of the Lamb. For the Lamb at the center of the throne will be their shepherd. (Rev. 7:15, 17)

Can it be that the Creator of all the galaxies was also named the Lamb? The gentle creature of whom the poet asked:

Little lamb, who made thee?
Dost thou know who made thee?
Gave thee life, and bid thee feed
By the stream and o'er the mead,
Gave thee clothing of delight,
Softest clothing, woolly, bright;
Gave thee such a tender voice,
Making all the vales rejoice?
Little lamb, who made thee?
Dost thou know who made thee?
Little lamb, I'll tell thee,
Little lamb, I'll tell thee.
He is called by thy name,
For He calls Himself a Lamb.
He is meek, and He is mild,
He became a little child.
I a child, and thou a lamb,
We are called by His name.

Little lamb, God bless thee!
Little lamb, God bless thee!

—WILLIAM BLAKE, *Songs of Innocence*

The lamb, even today, symbolizes innocence and purity. Only a pure unblemished lamb could be a sacrifice. A spotted lamb was not acceptable. The sacrificial lamb could not have any flaw or deformity. It could not harbor a parasite or suffer from any ailment. It had to be the firstborn of its mother.

The offering of a lamb had to be from an obedient heart in order to be acceptable. This was true of the very first offering mentioned in Scripture—Abel's offering of a lamb from his flock (Gen. 4)—and continues to be true for every offering thereafter. King Saul's proposed offering was rejected because he had been disobedient (1 Sam. 15). He was told, "To obey is better than sacrifice, and to heed is better than the fat of rams" (v. 22). The offering of the Lamb was an offering of obedience. The writer of Hebrews says of Christ, the Lamb, "Although he was a son, he learned obedience from what he suffered" (5:8).

For the offering to be complete, the blood of the Lamb had to be shed. "And without the shedding of blood there is no forgiveness" (Heb 9:22).

All the animals sacrificed in the time of the Old Testament were object lessons, pointing toward the one sufficient, worthy sacrifice. Because all of us have sinned, the only One who could provide an acceptable sacrifice was God himself. Abraham was more right than he knew when he told Isaac, "God himself will provide the lamb for the burnt offering" (Gen. 22:8).

God's Lamb, holy, pure, perfect, and altogether worthy, shed his blood as an offering to atone for our sins. For us, the Creator of the galaxies became a Child, who became the Lamb of God.

The wonder is that "we are called by His name"! What does it mean for me, today, that I am called a lamb? What does it mean for me, today, that Jesus is the Lamb?

"Worthy is the Lamb, who was slain, to receive power and wealth and wisdom and strength and honor and glory and praise!" (Rev. 5:12)

Worthy Lamb of God, receive our praise and gratitude today for your great sacrifice on our behalf.

Having never sinned, Jesus was a sacrifice willing
and able to redeem us from our sins. Extravagant love
motivated his sacrifice. Use the lines below to write
out a simple response to his extravagant love.

23

IMMANUEL— GOD WITH US

Scripture: Matthew 1:18–25

The virgin will be with child and will give birth to a son, and they will call him Immanuel—which means, "God with us." (Matt. 1:23) *mmanuel means a restored relationship.* When sin entered the world, there was a real sense in which the holy God was prevented from being with the men and women God had created. The God-man had to come in order to bring about a reconciliation. It is because of the death and resurrection of the Immanuel that we can know that God is with us.

Immanuel means there is One who knows how we feel, who identifies with us. Sometimes God gives us a hint of his kind of empathy through another person. For example, a young mother had ventured out to the grocery store with her three small children. It was her first such trip after the birth of her third baby. As she approached the checkout lanes, the three-year-old managed to knock a large jar of grape jelly onto the floor, leaving in her wake a huge puddle of broken glass and gooey grape jelly. The five-year-old announced in no uncertain terms that she had to go to the bathroom, now. The baby's wails announced loudly to the entire store that he was hungry. Every checkout lane had a long line of shoppers with heavily laden carts. A woman at the head of one of the lanes steered the young mother in front of her.

"You go first," she said. "I have five children of my own, and I know how you feel."

Immanuel means we don't have to feel alone. There is often an aloneness that comes even in the midst of a large crowd of people—just ask any young child who has ever been lost in such a crowd. There is the aloneness of being misunderstood. There is the aloneness of being in an empty house or apartment, all by oneself, night after night. And there is the aloneness of trying to carry a heavy load without help.

God With Us, your promise, first offered in the darkest of times, gave hope. And you are still with us in our darkest times. Our hearts are grateful to you, Immanuel.

God knows the intimate details of our lives—our suffering, our joys, our struggles. God pays great attention to the details, even "numbering the hairs on your head" (Matt. 10:30, THE MESSAGE). List a concern that has seemed too inconsequential to bring up in prayer. Ask God to intercede and come to your aid. Remember: He delights in relationship with you.

24

POTTER

Scripture: Isaiah 64:8; Jeremiah 18:6; Romans 9:21; Ephesians 2:10; 2 Corinthians 4:7

You are the **potter**; we are all the work of your hand. (Isa. 64:8)

"O house of Israel, can I not do with you as this **potter** does?" declares the LORD. "Like clay in the hand of the **potter**, so are you in my hand." (Jer. 18:6)

*O*uch! I don't like the way you're pressing and squeezing me! . . .

That's to work the air bubbles out, you say? So I won't crack later on? Oh . . .

You wouldn't *throw* me on that moving wheel, would you? It's spinning so fast; I'm not ready for anything like that yet . . .

But you're ready? And that's all that matters? Hmmm . . .

Hey! This hurts! Don't you think about my feelings at all? . . .

Check out the scars in the Potter's hands . . . What kind of an answer is that anyway? . . .

I don't think I like being this shape. And while we're on that subject, the color of the glaze you've chosen for me isn't at all becoming, if you ask me . . .

You didn't ask me? Oh . . .

Surely you aren't going to make me just another ordinary water pot, are you? I had so hoped to be something unique—a priceless *objet d'art* . . .

Wait a minute! You weren't planning to put me in the kiln, were you? It's hot in there! Why, if I do get out of that oven, I won't ever be the same again! . . .

That was your plan, you say? To make me strong and usable? A jar to hold living water? That the excellency of the power may be of God and not of . . . oh. I think I'm beginning to see.

> But who are you, a mere human being, to talk back to God? Shall what is formed say to the one who formed it, "Why did you make me like this?" Does not the potter have the right to make out of the same lump of clay some pottery for noble purposes and some for disposal of refuse?
>
> (Rom. 9:20–21 TNIV).

POTTER

Have thine own way, Lord! Have thine own way!
Thou are the Potter; I am the clay.
Mold me and make me, after thy will,
While I am waiting, yielded and still.

—ADELAIDE A. POLLARD, 1902

Master Potter, I place myself into your loving hands to mold me and make me according to your divine plan for my life.

This vivid metaphor from Scripture reminds us to yield to God's unique and masterful design for our lives. Recall a time when you fought God's will for your life. What was the result? Now write about something you're struggling to surrender to God today. A good prayer might be, "Lord, I believe; help my unbelief" (Mark 9:23–25).

25

ABBA, FATHER

Scripture: Luke 15:11–31

You received the Spirit of sonship. And by him we cry, "Abba, Father." The Spirit himself testifies with our spirit that we are God's children. Now if we are children, then we are heirs—heirs of God and co-heirs with Christ. (Rom. 8:15–17)

This, then, is how you should pray: "Our Father in heaven, hallowed be your name." (Matt. 6:9)

When Israel was a child, I loved him, and out of Egypt I called my son. It was I who taught Ephraim to walk, taking them by the arms. (Hos. 11:1, 3)

Be imitators of God, therefore, as dearly loved children. (Eph. 5:1)

Fatherhood is initiated by the act of the father, not the child. No child can choose their own father. In the same way, our relationship with our heavenly Father exists because he took the initiative.

Fathers often have children who resemble them. That is how it should be with our heavenly Father. In human relationships, children may look like their fathers because they share some of the same genes and chromosomes. Our heavenly Father has created us in his own image. So we resemble him in a way his other creatures do not. In addition, little children watch their fathers and become like them by imitating them. Children learn to copy mannerisms, speech patterns, and other habits. They may try on a parent's shoes or clothing in order to be like the parent. They learn to value what the parent values. In much the same way, we who are God's children are to imitate and to work at becoming children who resemble their Father.

A father is accessible to his child. A busy and important business executive has an outer office where secretaries screen his calls and where visitors wait. They may enter the inner office only after they are properly announced. But when the executive's young child arrives on the scene, the formalities are dispensed with. The child calls out "Daddy!" excitedly, toddles in, and plops down on the father's lap. Our heavenly Father has made himself accessible to us. We need not wait to be announced or to have our credentials checked. He is always ready to hear us and to converse with us.

A father's child is usually his heir. The heir is the one who is legally entitled to receive what has belonged to the father. Think of all that belongs to our heavenly Father! Because of our relationship with him, we are entitled to receive it! As the apostle Paul put it, "Now if we are children, then we are heirs—heirs of God and co-heirs with Christ" (Rom. 8:17).

The father loves his child. There are human fathers who don't love their children. Sometimes God puts in our path the child of such a person, and we have the opportunity to love that child with a fatherlike love. Without a human example, such a child has a hard time seeing God as a Father. Some of us have been blessed with human fathers who do love us dearly. We have been given an object lesson, a hint of what being loved by the heavenly Father is like!

Our loving Father longs to teach us how to walk. "It was I who taught Ephraim to walk, taking them by the arms," writes the prophet Hosea of the Father God (11:3). The love of our heavenly Father is not based on what we can do for him. It is not conditioned on our perfect obedience. It is a love that allows us to make our own mistakes so that we may grow from them. It is a love that will discipline us so we will become the people we were created to be. The Father's love is something we cannot seek, earn, buy, or deserve. It is a love that desires the very best for us and knows what that best is. "Every good and perfect gift is from above, coming down from the Father of the heavenly lights, who does not change like shifting shadows" (James 1:17).

> Fatherlike, he tends and spares us,
> Well our feeble frame he knows;
> In his hands he gently bears us,
> Rescues us from all our foes;
> Praise him, praise him,
> Praise him, praise him,
> Widely as his mercy goes.
>
> —HENRY F. LYTE, 1834 (BASED ON PSALM 103)

Our Father in heaven, hallowed be your name!

Human fathers are imperfect. Our relationships with them are often complicated. But one thing is for sure: our heavenly Father is perfect and his love for us is pure and loving. Write down a couple of characteristics of pure, loving parenthood. On the lines below, offer up thanks to God for his perfect, gracious way of parenting us.

26

CREATOR

Scripture: Psalm 8; Isaiah 40:25–26, 28

"To whom will you compare me? Or who is my equal?"
says the Holy One. Lift your eyes and look to the
heavens: Who **created** all these? He who brings out
the starry host one by one, and calls them each by
name. Because of his great power and mighty strength,
not one of them is missing. Do you not know? Have
you not heard? The LORD is the everlasting God, the
Creator of the ends of the earth. (Isa. 40:25–26, 28)

*W*e like to think we are creative, and indeed we are prolific makers of things. Were we to consider the last hundred years alone, a listing of the human inventions that facilitate transportation, communication, and generally make life easier would fill a book.

To create is "to cause to exist, to bring into being." God alone can truly cause something to exist. God alone can take meaningless nothing, without form and void, and make of it something significant.

It is because we have indeed been created in God's image that we have the capacity to take what we have been given and form from it something fresh.

The conception and subsequent birth of a child is a glorious, creative act that God allows us to participate in. But who really caused that child to exist? Who really brought that child into being?

Using the gifts God has put at our disposal, we as God's image-bearers paint, we compose or perform music, we sculpt, we write, we weave, we knit, we cook, we sew, and sometimes we come up with something that has a fresh sound or a fresh look to it. Our work went into "creation," and people sometimes laud our efforts as creative or imaginative. But the best creations of the image bearers are at most reminders of, and reflections of, our Creator.

> The spacious firmament on high,
> With all the blue ethereal sky,
> And spangled heav'ns, a shining frame,
> Their great Original proclaim.
> Th' unwearied sun, from day to day,
> Does his Creator's pow'r display,
> And publishes to ev'ry land
> The work of an almighty hand.

Soon as the evening shades prevail,
The moon takes up the wondrous tale,
And nightly to the list'ning earth
Repeats the story of her birth;
Whilst all the stars that round her burn,
And all the planets in their turn,
Confirm the tidings as they roll,
And spread the truth from pole to pole.

What though, in solemn silence, all
Move round this dark terrestrial ball?
What though nor real voice nor sound
Amidst their radiant orbs be found?
In reason's ear they all rejoice,
And utter forth a glorious voice;
For ever singing as they shine,
"The hand that made us is divine."

—JOSEPH ADDISON, 1712 (BASED ON PSALM 19)

Creator God, forgive us for clinging so foolishly to that which we consider "our" creation. Help us to lay these creations and the recognition or lack of recognition they bring us at the feet of the only One truly worthy of the name Creator.

Consider for a moment a few of the greatest works of humanity that you've ever witnessed, for instance, a painting, an architectural wonder, or even a technological marvel. Now consider how that created thing came to be. Can you trace the line between that great "created" work back to the Ultimate Creator, God? Take a moment to write a prayer of wonder in the lines below.

27

LION OF THE TRIBE OF JUDAH

Scripture: Job 10:16; Jeremiah 49:19;
Ezekiel 19:1–4; Hosea 5:14–15; 11:9–10;
13:4–8; Amos 3:4; Revelation 5:5

Like a **lion** coming up from Jordan's thickets to a rich pastureland, I [the LORD] will chase Edom from its land in an instant . . . Who is like me and who can challenge me? And what shepherd can stand against me? (Jer. 49:19)

Then one of the elders said to me, "Do not weep! See, the **Lion of the tribe of Judah** . . . has triumphed. He is able to open the scroll and its seven seals." (Rev. 5:5)

*T*he King of Beasts! Majestic, powerful, beautiful, awful. We shudder at his roar. We shiver to think of the potential of those claws and teeth. He must never be considered tame.

The One named Lion of the tribe of Judah is the same One the prophet Ezekiel wrote about:

> What a lioness was your mother
>> among the lions!
> She lay down among the young lions
>> and reared her cubs. (19:2)

She nursed them, chased off intruders, and taught them all the ways of a lion.

> She brought up one of her cubs,
>> and he became a strong lion.
> He learned to tear the prey
>> and he devoured men. (19:3)

We are the Lion's adopted cubs—we have been fed, protected, and taught.

Unchallengeable, the Lion chased away his enemies in an instant. No mere shepherd dares stand against him (Jer. 49:19). And we are the Lion's cubs!

The Lion's cubs forget who feeds them and become proud. Since cubs are the privileged progeny of the Lion, they are the ones he loves enough to punish. The Lion destroys his enemies but punishes his cubs so that "in their misery they will earnestly seek [him]" (Hos. 5:15).

Sometimes a cub holds his head high, thinking for a moment that he is the King instead of the cub. At such a time, the Lion stalks his own cub and again displays his awesome power (Job 10:16).

C. S. Lewis, in his *Chronicles of Narnia*, paints a wonderful picture of Aslan, the Great Lion:

"Ooh!" said Susan, "I'd thought he was a man. Is he—quite safe? I shall feel rather nervous about meeting a lion."

"That you will, dearie, and no mistake," said Mrs. Beaver. "If there's anyone who can appear before Aslan without their knees knocking, they're either braver than most, or just silly."

"Then he isn't safe?" said Lucy.

"Safe?" said Mr. Beaver. "Don't you hear what Mrs. Beaver tells you? Who said anything about safe? 'Course he isn't safe. But he's good. He's the King, I tell you."[4]

Good and terrible Lion, "You are worthy . . . to receive glory and honor and power, for you created all things, and by your will they were created and have their being."
(Rev. 4:11)

The image of God as a lion can make us feel nervous because lions are so powerful. That's why this image is apt. God's glory and power are great! Scripture reminds us that "the fear of the LORD is the beginning of wisdom" (Proverbs 9:10). In what ways do you fear the Lord? How does that fear lead to wisdom?

28

A CONSUMING FIRE

Scripture: Malachi 3:1–4

Our God is **a consuming fire**. (Heb. 12:29)

Then suddenly the Lord you are seeking will come to his temple . . . But who can endure the day of his coming? Who can stand when he appears? For he will be like a refiner's **fire** . . . He will sit as a refiner and purifier of silver; he will purify the Levites and refine them like gold and silver. Then the LORD will have men who will bring offerings in righteousness. (Mal. 3:1–3)

By day the LORD went ahead of them in a pillar of cloud to guide them on their way and by night in a pillar of **fire** to give them light, so they could travel by day or night. Neither the pillar of cloud by day nor the pillar of **fire** by night left its place in front of the people. (Ex. 13:21–22)

*T*he neon lights of our city streets pale in comparison to the brilliance of God. No human invention could have lit up the sky like God's towering inferno!

The pillar of fire, although it was probably regarded with reverence, did not strike terror in the hearts of the Israelites who saw it. A mother, putting her little one to bed, could provide assurance to her child. The fiery night-light at the entrance of the camp meant that God himself was with them, watching as they slept. If ever the desert night grew chill, God's fire was their warmth. Sometimes night travel was a welcome relief from travel during the desert's daytime heat. The fiery pillar would lead the way, showing the Israelites where they were to go. They did not need to carry torches. The pillar of fire provided light and direction. Every night God's fire would be there with them. His people could count on it. The pillar of fire was their comfort.

The God who is a comforting fire is also a consuming fire. The fire of God fell from heaven and utterly devoured the water-drenched sacrifice of God's prophet, Elijah (1 Kings 18:38).

Our God is also like a refiner's fire. Only a very small percentage of each chunk of ore is pure gold. The ore is full of impurities. To extract the gold so that it can be used, the ore must be placed in a furnace and subjected to tremendous temperatures. At last, the once-solid ore melts, and the gold can be separated.

There is a comforting aspect to this Consuming Fire. It is not the sons of Jacob the Cheat who are consumed (Mal. 3:6)—it is their impurity and sin. Being melted and having all but the gold stripped away, then being melted again and shaped—it is a painful process. But the Refiner knows what he is about.

> When through fiery trials thy pathway shall lie,
> My grace, all sufficient, shall be thy supply.

The flame shall not hurt thee; I only design
Thy dross to consume, and thy gold to refine.

—"K" in Rippon's *Selection*, 1787

What can be our response? The writer of Hebrews suggests, "Let us be thankful, and so worship God acceptably with reverence and awe, for our 'God is a consuming fire'" (Heb. 12:28–29).

God of Consuming Fire, you who burn away our impurities, you who light our way, you who warm our hearts, receive our gratitude this day.

Fire can provide light and warmth, and it can purify. How has God embodied those three characteristics in your life recently?

29

MAN OF SORROWS

Scripture: Isaiah 53

He was despised and rejected by men, **a man of sorrows,** and familiar with suffering. Like one from whom men hide their faces he was despised, and we esteemed him not. (Isa. 53:3)

*T*he process of being booked is completely depersonalizing. One's wallet, watch, and other possessions are confiscated. Often one's own clothing must be exchanged for institutional garb. Fingerprinting is required. Even one's own name must be exchanged for an identifying number. This impersonal number must be held high while the police photographer takes mug shots. The details are placed in the official police record. The one who is booked is now numbered with the transgressors.

The Man of Sorrows was "numbered with the transgressors" (Isa. 53:12). In the divine record, he was booked for all the sins of all humankind. He understands well the stigma and the humiliation attached.

> He was despised and rejected by men, a man of sorrows, and familiar with suffering. Like one from whom men hide their faces . . . (Isa. 53:3)

Worse still, the Man of Sorrows knows the indescribable horror of having God hide his face. "My God, my God, why have you forsaken me?" he cried (Matt. 27:46).

Playwright Thornton Wilder spoke more truth than perhaps he realized when in *Our Town* he wrote, "In love's service, only the wounded can serve." The Man of Sorrows came to be pierced, crushed, and wounded (Isa. 53:5). And he came because he loved us.

The suffering, the sorrow, and the wounds we sometimes experience pale in contrast to those of the Man of Sorrows. It hardly seems appropriate to use the same words to describe them. But the Man of Sorrows doesn't turn from us. He knows what we feel. He, of all who ever walked this earth, knows how to empathize with us. He became sin for us, and in so doing, our tears became his tears; our grief, his grief; and our pain, his pain. And "by his wounds we are healed" (Isa. 53:5). He took the permanence out of pain.

> Man of Sorrows! What a name
> For the Son of God, who came
> Ruined sinners to reclaim;
> Hallelujah! What a Savior!
>
> Bearing shame and scoffing rude,
> In my place condemned he stood,
> Sealed my pardon with his blood.
> Hallelujah! What a Savior!
>
> Guilty, vile, and helpless, we;
> Spotless Lamb of God was he;
> Full atonement! Can it be?
> Hallelujah! What a Savior!
>
> Lifted up was he to die,
> "It is finished!" was his cry:
> Now in heaven exalted high:
> Hallelujah! What a Savior!
>
> When he comes, our glorious King,
> All his ransomed home to bring;
> Then anew this song we'll sing:
> Hallelujah! What a Savior!
>
> —PHILIP P. BLISS (1838–1876)

Man of Sorrows, we kneel before you this day and exclaim, "What a Savior!"

The prophet foretold that the Messiah would be "a man of suffering, familiar with pain" (Isaiah 53). Jesus suffered greatly, but he also experienced great joy. He promised that his followers would share his joy and that "it would be full" (John 15:11). Write a line or two about your suffering with Jesus, then share something that brings you great joy. He longs to share your joy!

30

EL SHADDAI

Scripture: Genesis 43:14; Psalm 131:2–3

When Abram was ninety-nine years old, the LORD appeared to him and said, "I am God Almighty [El Shaddai] . . . I have made you a father of many nations. I will make you very fruitful; I will make nations of you, and kings will come from you." (Gen. 17:1, 5–6)

And may God Almighty [El Shaddai] grant you mercy before the man so that he will let your other brother and Benjamin come back with you. (Gen. 43:14)

Because of your father's God [the el], who helps you, because of the Almighty [Shaddai], who blesses you with blessings of the heavens above, blessings of the deep that lies below, blessings of the breast and womb. (Gen. 49:25)

But Zion said, "The LORD has forsaken me, the LORD has forgotten me." Can a mother forget the baby at her breast and have no compassion on the child she has borne? Though she may forget, I will never forget you! See, I have engraved you on the palms of my hands. (Isa. 49:14–16)

> But I have stilled and quieted my soul;
>> like a weaned child with its mother,
>> like a weaned child is my soul within me.
> O Israel, put your hope in the LORD. (Ps. 131:2–3)

O Jerusalem, Jerusalem, you who kill the prophets and stone those sent to you, how often I have longed to gather your children together, as a hen gathers her chicks under her wings, but you were not willing. (Matt. 23:37)

*I*n somewhat the same way as God is bigger than any and all of the names we can name him, he is also bigger than the images our minds conjure of a single gender. Scripture, in showing us facets of who God is, sometimes portrays God in terms we associate with the feminine gender.

The Hebrew name *El Shaddai* comes as close to capturing this aspect of God as does any of his names. The traditional translations of Scripture have consistently rendered this name "Almighty." But to appreciate its full flavor, it will be helpful to examine its Hebrew roots.[5] *El* is a shortened form of *Elohim*. It sets forth the might, the strength, and the excellence of God. *Shad* is the Hebrew word for "breast." *Shaddai* pictures God's fullness or bounty, his tenderness, his generosity, his desire to nurture us and make us fruitful. In one name, God's attributes of might and tenderness are brought together!

When Abram was ninety-nine years old, El Shaddai appeared to him and said, "I have made you a father" (Gen. 17:5). Speaking in strictly human terms, it takes a woman to go to a man and say, "I'm going to make you a father!" Sometimes this announcement comes as a shock. Often the shocking aspect of this news is mingled with a great deal of joy and thanksgiving, along with some apprehension. Certainly all of these emotions were present as El Shaddai's announcement was received. "You will be very fruitful—nations and kings will come from you" (Gen. 17:6, paraphrase).

It was Elohim Shaddai who gave birth to the nation of Israel. The prophet Isaiah described the birthing process thus: "Like a woman in childbirth I cry out, I gasp and pant" (42:14).

Jacob is full of anxiety as he is about to send his beloved son Benjamin off to Egypt in response to the whimsical demand of the ruler who dispensed food. "May [El Shaddai] grant you mercy before the man," he cries (Gen. 43:14).

Later, as Jacob is pronouncing God's blessing on his son Joseph, he says, "Because of the El and the Shaddai, may you have blessings of the breast and the womb" (Gen. 49:25, paraphrase).

Isaiah, in describing the love of God, says it is greater than that of a nursing mother. A unique bonding occurs as the mother holds her child close to her breast. She is the source of all the infant needs for nourishment as she holds the child close to the warmth of her body, within the sound of her heartbeat and secure in the safety of her arms.

A further dimension to this picture is added by the psalmist in Psalm 131. The psalmist feels like a weaned child. "*Why* am I being deprived of what, from my point of view, seems so good and so right?" he may have been asking himself. "This is what I need, God. Why can't I have it?"

Have you ever asked God these sorts of questions?

God, who, like a mother, knows that the growing child must move beyond breast milk, still holds the child close enough to hear the divine heartbeat, allowing the child the warmth and security of being held tightly in divine arms.

Children's questions may still be unanswered. But their souls are stilled and quieted "like a weaned child with its mother" (Ps. 131:2), because they know, without any doubt, who is holding them!

El Shaddai, almighty, tender God, hold us close to your heart today.

This ancient name shows God simultaneously mighty and tender. Imagine God's firm, loving hand on your back right now, leading you with intention and ultimate goodwill. Lean into God's strength and kindness. How does that make you feel?

31

ADVOCATE

Scripture: Hebrews 2:16; 4:15–16

My little children, I am writing this to you so that
you may not sin; but if any one does sin, we have an
advocate with the Father, Jesus Christ the righteous.
(1 John 2:1 RSV)

*W*hat if you had to stand before the great eternal Judge and present your own case? Imagine yourself, standing alone at the bar, clothed in your own very best efforts. The prosecutor is a shrewd one. He has all the resources of hell itself to draw on. The key exhibit in this case is your own obedience to the law of God. What would the verdict be?

Scripture leaves no room for question. "All have sinned and fall short of the glory of God," writes the apostle Paul (Rom. 3:23). Guilty.

But we don't have to present our own case. We have an Advocate, one who stands in our place to speak on our behalf. Our Advocate has the necessary qualifications. He is familiar with our case and has been since before the earth was founded (Isa. 40:21–28).

Our Advocate prepares his clients. He knows that, dressed in our own righteousness, we don't stand a chance. At great personal cost, he has seen to it that appropriate clothing has been provided to us.

A certain defendant awaited the day of his trial in jail. He was scheduled to appear before a judge who was known for his fastidious attention to proper courtroom dress and decorum. Male defendants who appeared before him were expected to wear a coat and tie. But this defendant did not own a coat or tie and had no means of procuring them. Before the appointed hour of the trial, the defendant received the appropriate clothing, specially delivered to him. The clothing had been sent by the judge himself, from his personal wardrobe.

When we stand before God, we will be able to stand there in clothing provided from the Judge's own wardrobe. We will be able to wear the righteousness of God himself!

When we stand before God, we will not need to stand alone. Our Advocate, Jesus Christ the Righteous, will be standing with us. He will plead our case, and already we can rejoice in the verdict.

> My advocate appears for my defense on high;
> The Father bows his ears and lays his thunder by.
> Not all that hell or sin can say
> Shall turn his heart, his love away.
>
> —Isaac Watts, 1709

Jesus, our Advocate, our case is totally without merit, except that we may claim your righteousness. Stand with us today!

If you had an unlimited access to a top-notch law firm and unlimited budget to spend, what would you do with their advocacy? What battles would you want those attorneys to fight on your behalf? Now remember you have an eternal Advocate who fights for you. What requests do you have for the Ultimate Advocate?

32

FAITHFUL WITNESS

Scripture: Revelation 1:1–6; John 1:1–3; 11:25 14:6, 9;
1 Corinthians 15:55–57; Ephesians 2:12–13; Acts 1:8

Grace and peace to you . . . from Jesus Christ, who is
the faithful witness, the firstborn from the dead, and
the ruler of the kings of the earth. (Rev. 1:5)

*W*hat is a good witness? A good witness is someone who was there. Someone who can accurately and faithfully attest to what he or she experienced, saw, tasted, and felt. A good witness often has a credible record, someone who has proven reliable in the past. A good witness will often impact the verdict.

Translators of Scripture ordinarily consider the oldest manuscripts to be the most reliable. They look for the testimony closest in time to the event or statement. But there is nothing secondhand or circumstantial about the testimony of Jesus Christ, Faithful Witness. The apostle John indicates at the beginning of his gospel that this witness was present with God from the beginning. He testifies to the whole truth of God, and nothing but the truth. We can count on this testimony to be faithful and accurate. When this witness assures us that whoever believes in him will live, even though he dies, that testimony has the ring of authenticity. For this witness has felt the sting of death. The dead body of this witness was buried. Then this witness, himself, was the first to be raised from the dead.

Jesus Christ, Faithful Witness, has signed his word in blood. This has impacted the verdict! We are freed from our sins. And there is even more: we are no longer illegal aliens but kingdom citizens.

We are priests, John continues as he relates the testimony of this witness. What does that mean for us? It means we have access at any time to the presence of the God we serve. We require no special introduction, and we need not schedule an appointment through some secretary.

In the person of this witness we see the face of the God who loves us. Because of his reliability in the past, we can trust him concerning our future. His Spirit even empowers us to be witnesses on his behalf!

You, Jesus Christ, are the Faithful Witness! You are the reliable word. To you be glory and power forever and ever!

Perspective matters. When police interview witnesses to a crime, each might remember the scene differently with varying degrees of accuracy. Sometimes our memories fail us. Scripture reminds us we have a "Faithful Witness" in Jesus. He accurately testifies to us about the love of God. His Word is infinitely reliable. Think of three truths his Word has taught you and list them here.

33

BRIDEGROOM

Scripture: Isaiah 62:5

As a **bridegroom** rejoices over his bride, so will your God rejoice over you. (Isa. 62:5)

The bride belongs to the **bridegroom**. The friend who attends the **bridegroom** waits and listens for him, and is full of joy when he hears the **bridegroom's** voice. That joy is mine, and it is now complete. (John 3:29)

*I*n our twenty-first-century society, traditional weddings tend to focus on the bride. Traditionally, the bride's family issues the invitations, plans and pays for the reception, and hosts the wedding. When the wedding processional begins, all eyes look in the direction of the approaching bride. Few even notice, until after the fact, that the groom has also entered to the accompaniment of the same music!

But a marriage ceremony was very different in Middle Eastern cultures during the time when the Scriptures were being written.

The bridegroom and his family hosted the wedding. This is clear from the account of the wedding at Cana, where Jesus did his first miracle (John 2:1–11)—the bridegroom supplied the wine. It is also indicated in a parable Jesus told (Matt. 22:2). A king prepared a wedding banquet for his son. The wedding invitations were personally delivered by servants from the bridegroom's household.

The bridegroom is the key figure in the wedding procession (Matt. 25:1–10). All the attendants are to be in readiness for the bridegroom's arrival. The psalmist compares the sun to "a bridegroom coming forth from his pavilion" (Ps. 19:5). The bridegroom's arrival is a glorious moment, and from that point on, the excitement crescendos.

The bridegroom has gone to great personal expense and effort in order that this wedding could take place. In preparation, "a bridegroom adorns his head like a priest" (Isa. 61:10). A priest's head was anointed with oil as a symbol that he was set apart for the special purpose of offering sacrifices to God on behalf of the people. Our Bridegroom, Jesus Christ, is worthy of the adornment of a priest. He has offered the supreme sacrifice— himself—on behalf of his bride.

Our Bridegroom has even provided clothing for the bride to wear: "fine linen, bright and clean" (Rev. 19:8).

> The bride eyes not her garment, but her dear
> bridegroom's face;
> [She] will not gaze at glory, but on [her] King of grace;
> Not at the crown He gifteth, but on His pierced hand:
> The Lamb is all the glory of Emmanuel's land.
> —ANNE R. COUSIN, 1857, BASED UPON SAMUEL RUTHERFORD
> (1600–1661)

The wedding supper will certainly be the wedding feast to end all wedding feasts. The angel who described the plans for the celebration to the apostle John said that those who were invited were blessed (Rev. 19:9).

There will be a great multitude at this wedding, all at the invitation of the Father of the Bridegroom, God himself! They will greet the arrival of the Bridegroom with shouting that sounds like the roar of rushing waters and peals of loud thunder.

> Hallelujah!
> For our Lord God Almighty reigns.
> Let us rejoice and be glad
> and give him glory!
> For the wedding of the Lamb has come,
> and his bride has made herself ready.
> (REV. 19:6–7)

O Jesus Christ, our Bridegroom! Help us to prepare for your coming with the meticulous care of a bride-to-be. Help us to anticipate your coming with the enthusiasm of a bride-to-be. Come, Lord Jesus.

Consider the happy anticipation that precedes the arrival of loved ones—those who love us just as much as we love them, if not more! The image of Bridegroom prompts us to consider how we are preparing ourselves for our ultimate Loved One's arrival. What special steps might you take today to prepare?

34

PRINCE OF PEACE

Scripture: Ephesians 2:11–18

And he will be called . . . **Prince of Peace**. (Isa. 9:6)

And the **peace** of God, which transcends all understanding, will guard your hearts and your minds in Christ Jesus. (Phil. 4:7)

Peace I leave with you; my peace I give you. I do not give to you as the world gives. Do not let your hearts be troubled and do not be afraid. (John 14:27)

I have told you these things, so that in me you may have **peace**. In this world you will have trouble. But take heart! I have overcome the world. (John 16:33)

But the fruit of the Spirit is . . . **peace**. (Gal. 5:22)

*S*ee if you can paint in your mind a picture of peace. Most of us will visualize a quiet, tranquil, well-ordered scene with an absence of any sort of conflict. But when we look at the picture of the Prince of Peace presented in Scripture, it shatters our mental images.

It is noteworthy that the very first promise of the One who would come and who would be called Prince of Peace states that "he will crush [Satan's] head" (Gen. 3:15). The apostle Paul picks up on this image in Romans 16:20: "The God of peace will soon crush Satan under your feet. The grace of our Lord Jesus be with you." Crushing someone underfoot is hardly a tranquil activity. The act of crushing seems more warlike than peaceful. Paul describes the believer by using the metaphor of a soldier putting on his armor in preparation for battle. The soldier's footwear is to be the "readiness that comes from the gospel of peace" (Eph. 6:15).

Perhaps one reason for the apparent contradiction is that we have lost some of the original Hebrew meaning for the word. The root of the Hebrew *shalom* or *shalam* (peace) may originally have signified oneness, completeness, or perfection.[6]

If peace involves perfection, is there hope for any of us? Listen to the words of Jesus: "Peace I leave with you; my peace I give you" (John 14:27). Christ Jesus offers us the perfection of his heart! God sees Christ's perfection and considers us perfect in him. Like a strong magnet pulls scattered bits of iron into line with itself, so his strong and perfect heart pulls our hearts into conformity with his.

In order to restore our oneness with God, in order to perfect us and make us complete, the greatest act of violence in all of history was committed. A superficial glossing over of the problem of sin would not have sufficed. God had to cut through to its very heart in order to purchase our peace.

He was pierced for our transgressions,
he was crushed for our iniquities;
the punishment that brought us peace was upon him,
and by his wounds we are healed. (Isa. 53:5)

The price of our peace was enormous.

The Prince of Peace did not come to smooth ruffled feathers. Not at the personal, national, or international level. His is a peace that starts in the heart and works its way outward, never the other way around. That is why it is a peace that "transcends all understanding" (Phil 4:7). The people around us look at the superficial circumstances that surround us. They can't understand what is going on in the heart of a child of God. Human understanding would have us believe that peace must work from the outside in.

The word *shalom* is even today used as a greeting by the Jewish people. The apostle Paul used it as a greeting and closing in most of his letters. And Jesus said, "Peace be with you" as he appeared to his assembled disciples after his death and resurrection (Luke 24:36). But when Jesus, Prince of Peace, uses the greeting *shalom*, it is far more than an intangible greeting or a wish. It is a gift. It is the gift of the Person who himself is Peace.

I am who you need. I am your perfection. I am your completeness. I am your reconciliation. I am your peace—this is the message of Jesus Christ, Prince of Peace.

The God of Peace is still engaged in less than tranquil activity, and we are still confronted with less than tranquil circumstances. But the price of our peace has already been paid. The promised Peace who has begun to work in the hearts of the children of God will one day work his way outward. The result will be that men will beat their swords into plowshares, and the lion will lie down with the lamb.

May the God of peace, who through the blood of the eternal covenant brought back from the dead our Lord Jesus, that great Shepherd of the sheep, equip [us] with everything good for doing his will, and may he work in us what is pleasing to him, through Jesus Christ, to whom be glory for ever and ever. (Heb. 13:20–21)

We are the happy recipients of the peace of Christ. Even so, we're often tempted into disrupting others' peace with our behavior or words. How might we sow peace today in the lives of those around us? List three ways you'll sow peace in the name of Jesus today.

35

LIVING BREAD

Scripture: John 6:1–14, 25–59; 1 Corinthians 11:23–24

Then Jesus declared, "I am the bread of life. He who comes to me will never go hungry." (John 6:35)

I am the living bread that came down from heaven. If anyone eats of this bread, he will live forever. This bread is my flesh, which I will give for the life of the world. (John 6:51)

The Lord Jesus, on the night he was betrayed, took bread, and when he had given thanks, he broke it and said, "This is my body, which is for you; do this in remembrance of me." (1 Cor. 11:23–24)

*B*read has been referred to as the staff of life. It is symbolic of the food we need for sustenance—not an optional food, such as pickles, artichokes, or chocolate. Bread is what supports us, nourishes us, and keeps us alive. The fragrance of freshly baked bread is an unspoken invitation few can resist.

In the late eighteenth century, the young queen of France, Marie Antoinette, became notorious for her extravagant lifestyle at a time when her government was facing financial crises. She is said to have one day asked an official why the Parisians were angry.

"They are hungry and have no bread," was the reply.

She has been remembered throughout two centuries for the insensitive response attributed to her: "Let them eat cake." Nourishment, not just something to fill them up, was what the French people needed.

What a contrast this attitude is to the one shown by Jesus (John 6). A great crowd had followed Jesus around the Sea of Galilee to see the miracles he was performing and to hear his teaching. There were no roadside fast-food restaurants for these people who had walked quite a distance from their homes.

"How shall we feed these people?" Jesus asked his disciples.

"You've got to be kidding," they responded. "We could spend eight months' salary and not have enough to give everyone in this crowd even a bite of bread."

One boy had thought ahead, or perhaps his mother had. He had brought a small lunch with him. Not much. But in the hands of the One who is the Living Bread, that small lunch provided an ample meal for well over five thousand people, with twelve baskets of leftovers.

"I am the bread of life," Jesus said later to some of the people who thought they had located a permanent free lunch ticket. Many didn't understand. They would be hungry again for the kind of food that spoils. But Jesus himself could supply them the kind of nourishment that would permanently quiet the spiritual hunger pangs each one had within. Just as people need bread for nourishment, so we need the sustenance Jesus supplies in order to live eternally.

A loaf of bread, golden brown and still warm from the oven, looks beautiful. But in order to do any good for anyone, it must be broken—first with hands or a knife, then with teeth. Finally, the body's digestive juices continue the "breaking down" process in order that the bread may do what it was meant to do.

Jesus, the Living Bread, also had to be broken in order to do what he was meant to do—be life for us. What Jesus offers is not cake—sweet, temporarily filling, but not particularly nourishing. Jesus offers bread—something both desirable and good for us. He offers to be for us what we need to live. He himself is the staff of life—eternal life.

Bread of Heaven, be for us our day's nourishment. You are who we need!

When we're hungry, an emptiness gnaws away at our bellies until we fill them. Spiritual hunger is worse. It's an ache that doesn't go away. Since Jesus is the Living Bread, we never have to experience spiritual emptiness again. How can we share Jesus with others, as he shared so freely? Write some ideas about sharing freely below.

36

THE WORD

Scripture: John 1:1–18; Revelation 19:11–16

In the beginning was the Word, and the Word was with God, and the Word was God. He was with God in the beginning. (John 1:1–2)

The Word became flesh and made his dwelling among us. We have seen his glory, the glory of the One and Only, who came from the Father, full of grace and truth. (John 1:14)

He is dressed in a robe dipped in blood, and his name is the Word of God. (Rev. 19:13)

*F*riends of a young man had told him about a girl they thought he should meet. They showed him a picture of her. He was interested, but many miles separated them. How could he get to know her at such a distance? He sent her a letter, telling her in his own words who he was, what he valued, and what his goals were. And she wrote back. The young man's most effective means of communicating what he was like was his word.

God has given us the testimony of friends. God has given us pictures—think of some of the names we have considered: Bread, Door, Star, Lamb. But his most effective expression of who he himself is, is his Word, Jesus Christ.

The right word enhances our understanding. It strips away the fog that surrounds a difficult or abstract concept. It can cut through a broad generality, making it clear that the speaker means A, not B or C.

The right word, from the right person, can be all that is necessary to establish credibility. "Give me your word, and I'll believe it."

The word is a reflection of what is in the heart. "Out of the overflow of [the] heart [the] mouth speaks," says Luke (6:45). The living Word was with God and was God from the beginning. He is the overflow of the abundant love that is the essence of the heart of God.

The living Word is God's best expression of himself. The Word clarifies who God is for us and enhances our understanding. The living Word is the best evidence for God's credibility.

Think of the power an ordinary word has in certain contexts: a jury foreman announces guilty; a young woman replies yes; the umpire calls strike; a congress declares war. The power of the living Word far exceeds the power of even these words. We need not fear a world filled with devils or the rage of the prince of darkness, for "one little Word shall fell him."

That Word above all earthly powers,
No thanks to them, abideth;
The Spirit and the gifts are ours
Through him who with us sideth;
Let goods and kindred go,
This mortal life also;
The body they may kill:
God's truth abideth still;
His kingdom is forever.

—MARTIN LUTHER, 1529

A word, once spoken, cannot be unsaid. God has expressed himself in the incarnate Word. He cannot and will not reverse himself. That Word is with us forever.

Come, thou Incarnate Word, Gird on thy mighty sword, Our prayer attend: Come and thy people bless, And give thy Word success . . . Amen.—Anonymous, c. 1757

Jesus as The Word means he is the expression of God—or the embodiment of—God's heart for us. Much as we express our love through words, God expressed (and continues to express) love for us through Jesus. Consider expressing love today with your words—maybe in a text or with a handwritten note. Write a loved one's name here along with a prompt of what you will say to express your feelings.

37

ROSE OF SHARON

Scripture: Song of Solomon 2:1

I am a rose of Sharon, a lily of the valleys. (Song 2:1)

The rose of Sharon is a large hibiscus shrub. It grows about twelve feet tall, has large three-lobed leaves, and a lovely rose, purple, white, or blue flower.

The uniqueness of the rose of Sharon lies in the fact that it blooms at an unlikely time and in unlikely places. The rose blossoms in the fall, when few other shrubs are in bloom. It grows well in unfavorable conditions and does not seem to be partial to the city or the country.

Unfavorable growing conditions? In our honest moments we sometimes marvel that the soil of our lives could produce anything beautiful. It is full of the stones of selfishness, the weeds of deceitfulness, and the acidity of our pride. Yet the Rose of Sharon persists, blooms, and grows, even when other plants are dormant.

> Lo, how a rose upspringing
> On tender root has grown:
> A rose by prophet's singing
> To all the world made known.
> The Rose 'midst winter's cold
> A lovely blossom bearing,
> In former days foretold.
>
> This Flow'r whose fragrance tender
> With sweetness fills the air,
> Dispels with glorious splendor
> The darkness everywhere.
> True Man, yet very God;
> From sin and death he saves us
> And lightens every load.
>
> —GERMAN AUTHOR, UNKNOWN (c. 1500)

Jesus, Rose of Sharon, you startle and amaze us by being present at unlikely times and in unlikely places. These are the times and places we most need to see you. Bloom in our hearts today so that the lives of those around us may be touched by the beauty and fragrance of your love. Those who know us will wonder that such poor soil could produce such a flower. They will know it is the tenacity of the flower, not the quality of the soil. Receive our praise!

In what ways has God startled and amazed you lately? Write about a particular surprise from God below.

38

HOLY, HOLY, HOLY

Scripture: Isaiah 6:1–8; Exodus 33:17–23; 1 Peter 1:15–16

Holy, holy, holy is the LORD Almighty; the whole earth is full of his glory. (Isa. 6:3)

Day and night they never stop saying: "Holy, holy, holy is the Lord God Almighty, who was, and is, and is to come." (Rev. 4:8)

*I*n all of Scripture this is the one name or attribute of God that is named three times in succession. The emphasis cannot be accidental. God is so named by the four living creatures in Revelation and by the seraphim in Isaiah's vision. There are other names of God that are much easier for us to think about. If we are honest, this one makes us a little squeamish.

As we look at this name of God, the nearer we approach, and the more clearly we see, the more uncomfortable we become. To look at God's holiness is something like looking with unshaded eyes directly at the sun. God told Moses that no one could see his face and live. God covered Moses with his hand and allowed him to see his back. Moses' face shone as a result of this encounter.

The early Israelites were so conscious of God's holiness that they would never speak God's name aloud, or write it, except in abbreviated form. We, on the other hand, sometimes are so casual that we lose the impact of what it means for the Holy, Holy, Holy God to make himself one with sinful human beings. No analogy can do justice to the reality of God's incarnation for the purpose of our atonement, but perhaps we can begin to think in the right direction if we imagine a beautifully and carefully made white wedding dress being drenched in the sewer. Or imagine your thirteen-year-old daughter being raped. But because God is God, the sewer and the rape did not ruin him.

Not only is God holy, but he expects us to be holy also (1 Peter 1:15–16). Sometimes it seems more socially acceptable to be a little less than holy. Being holy doesn't always sound like a lot of fun. Sometimes being holy seems like an impossible achievement. It would be, if we had to do it by ourselves!

We have met the Holy, Holy, Holy God. Such an encounter must have one of two results: blasphemy or worship. Isaiah worshiped. In Isaiah 6 he catches a glimpse of the Holy God in a service of worship that begins with adoration and praise. Isaiah confesses his sin and is then assured of God's pardon. The Word of the Lord is proclaimed and Isaiah responds. The outgrowth of his worship is service. Service that does not spring from having worshiped, as Isaiah's did, soon becomes meaningless.

Holy, Holy, Holy God, like Isaiah, when we are confronted with your holiness, we become more acutely aware of our own sinfulness. We acknowledge it and we confess it. Help us to forsake our sin, to the end that we may obey your command to be holy, even as you are holy.

Holy, Holy, Holy God in three persons. We are full of wonder that you have made atonement for our sin.

Holy, Holy, Holy God. With Isaiah, we respond to your word, "Here am I. Send me!" (Isa. 6:8).

God's holiness always provokes a response. What
has been your response when you've witnessed God's
awesome glory and power? How can you show your
respect and gratitude today?

39

FRIEND OF TAX COLLECTORS AND SINNERS

Scripture: Luke 7:34–50

The Son of Man came eating and drinking, and they say, "Here is . . . a friend of tax collectors and 'sinners.'" (Matt. 11:19)

But there is a friend who sticks closer than a brother. (Prov. 18:24)

Greater love has no one than this, that he lay down his life for his friends. (John 15:13)

*E*ven more hated than the Roman conquerors were the tax collectors. The tax collector was no foreigner. He might have had a farm just down the road. He might have been Uncle Ezra's second cousin. A greedy tax collector (and most of them were) could demand not only the revenue required by Rome but also an additional amount to line his own pockets. He could get away with this because he was backed by Roman soldiers, who could, if necessary, be very persuasive! Such a collector turned his back on his friends in exchange for cash and clout.

Yet as Jesus was passing through Jericho one day, it was a tax collector he singled out from the crowd. It was a tax collector with whom Jesus chose to have lunch. As a result of Jesus' gracious friendship, Zacchaeus the tax collector became a changed man (Luke 19:1–10).

Matthew, another tax collector, was chosen to be part of Jesus' inner circle. He was one of the twelve who walked, worked, watched, ate, slept, and lived with Jesus during his time of ministry on earth. This collector of taxes later used his record-keeping ability to become a chronicler of the life of Jesus, his friend.

Jesus also openly acquainted himself with sinners. In a culture which didn't view any woman very highly, Jesus befriended "used" women. One prostitute was overwhelmed by the compassion she had experienced and the forgiveness she knew she had received from God. This broken woman poured on Jesus' feet her tears of repentance, together with the costly perfume from her broken jar (Luke 7:36–50). She had been made whole.

Then there was the foreign woman who slept around. She came to the well for her daily water supply at a time when none of the other women would be there, probably because they would look down their noses at her. Jesus befriended this woman as well. She became a new person (John 4:1–26).

Fellow friends of Jesus! Look around you at the company we

are in! Prostitutes, cheaters, liars—Jesus even called Judas his friend (Matt. 26:50). Just as there is nothing we ourselves can do to be worthy of his friendship, so there is nothing we can do to make ourselves ineligible for it.

The friendship has been offered. Jesus has extended his nail-scarred hand to us. All we need do is take it, and like the tax collectors and sinners before us, we won't ever be the same!

Lord Jesus, today we join hands and hearts with the great company of sinners you have made your friends. Receive our gratitude, we pray.

Jesus went out of his way to make people feel welcome. The resulting scorn and shame he received from religious leaders didn't bother him. Do you identify most with the "tax collectors and sinners" or with the religious leaders of the day? Write your response below.

40

OMEGA

Scripture: Psalm 102:25–28; Psalm 46

I am . . . the Omega, . . . the Last, . . . the End. (Rev. 22:13)

But you [God] remain the same, and your years will never end. (Ps. 102:27)

*S*o much of that with which we involve ourselves has an end. We spend ourselves preparing for a special visitor or a special occasion. The visit always ends, and the occasion is soon over. Time itself has an end. But God? Why does our eternal God name himself with the last letter of the Greek alphabet, omega? What can the name *Omega* tell us about God?

Sometimes advertisers use the phrase "the last word in . . . [whatever they are trying to sell]." They wish to convey the idea that after we have investigated every other similar product, we will find this one to be superior. Nothing else can surpass it.

Sometimes a person is said to have had "the last word" in a discussion or debate. The idea is that after everyone else has had their say and has presented their best argument, this one's word prevailed.

What does it mean to belong to the Omega God? What does it mean to be part of the unending ending? C. S. Lewis gives us a hint as he concludes the last of his Chronicles of Narnia:

> For us this is the end of all the stories, and we can most truly say that they all lived happily ever after. But for them it was only the beginning of the real story. All their life in this world and all their adventures in Narnia had only been the cover and the title page: now at last they were beginning Chapter One of the Great Story, which no one on earth has read: which goes on forever: in which every chapter is better than the one before.[7]

Our chief end is to glorify God and to enjoy him *forever*, says the Westminster Catechism. Are we so immersed in our lives today that we never stop to think about what our worshiping will be like in 100 years? Or what it will be like in 1,000 years? Or how about 479,502 years from now?

Belonging to the Omega God means that our worship takes

on eternal significance. Our task of inviting others to worship—our families, our neighbors, our coworkers—takes on eternal significance. And our task of equipping ourselves and others to be better worshipers is eternally significant.

You who precede all, nothing and no one will ever surpass you! Omega God, when all other words have been spoken, your Word prevails!

Help us, Omega God—you who precede all beginnings and succeed all endings—help us to look beyond the needs and demands of today. Equip us to better worship you, Omega God, the Last, the everlasting One.

How do you think belonging to "Omega God" differs from what temporal endings suggest? What endings have you experienced that because of Omega God are really not ending?

APPENDIX

Join All the Glorious Names!

This is a listing, in alphabetical order, of the names of God and the Scripture passages where they are found. The names are from the New International Version (1984 edition), unless otherwise noted.

I am indebted to Virgil and Carol Olson of Pasadena, California, for their assistance in compiling this list.

Abba	Romans 8:15
Advocate	1 John 2:1 (KJV)
Almighty	Psalm 68:14
Alpha	Revelation 22:13
Amen	Revelation 3:14
Ancient of Days	Daniel 7:9
Anointed One	Psalm 2:2
Apostle and High Priest	Hebrews 3:1
Arm of the Lord	Isaiah 53:1
Author of Life	Acts 3:15
Author of Our Faith	Hebrews 12:2
Beginning and the End	Revelation 21:6
Blessed and Only Ruler	1 Timothy 6:15
Branch	Jeremiah 33:15
Bread of God	John 6:33

Bread of Life	John 6:35
Bridegroom	Isaiah 62:5
Bright Morning Star	Revelation 22:16
Chief Shepherd	1 Peter 5:4
Chosen One	Isaiah 42:1
Christ	Matthew 22:42
Christ Jesus Our Lord	Romans 6:23
Christ of God	Luke 9:20
Christ the Lord	Luke 2:11
Christ, the Son of the Living God	Matthew 16:16
Comforter	John 14:26 (KJV)
Commander	Isaiah 55:4
Consolation of Israel	Luke 2:25
Consuming Fire	Deuteronomy 4:24; Hebrews 12:29
Cornerstone	Isaiah 28:16
Counselor	John 14:26
Creator	1 Peter 4:19
Deliverer	Romans 11:26
Desired of All Nations	Haggai 2:7
Door	John 10:7 (KJV)
El Shaddai	Genesis 17:1 (HEBREW)
Eternal God	Deuteronomy 33:27
Everlasting Father	Isaiah 9:6
Exact Representation of His [God's] Being	Hebrews 1:3
Faithful and True	Revelation 19:11
Faithful Witness	Revelation 1:5
Father	Matthew 6:9
Firstborn Among Many Brothers	Romans 8:29
Firstborn from the Dead	Revelation 1:5

Firstborn Over All Creation	Colossians 1:15
Firstfruits	1 Corinthians 15:20, 23
Foundation	1 Corinthians 3:11
Friend of Tax Collectors and "Sinners"	Matthew 11:19
Gentle Whisper	1 Kings 19:12
Gift of God	John 4:10
Glory of the Lord	Isaiah 40:5
God	Genesis 1:1
God Almighty	Genesis 17:1
God Over All	Romans 9:5
God Who Sees Me	Genesis 16:13
Good Shepherd	John 10:11
Great High Priest	Hebrews 4:14
Great Shepherd	Hebrews 13:20
Guide	Psalm 48:14
Head of the Body	Colossians 1:18
Head of the Church	Ephesians 5:23
Heir of All Things	Hebrews 1:2
High Priest Forever	Hebrews 6:20
Holy One	Acts 2:27
Holy One of Israel	Isaiah 49:7
Holy Spirit	John 14:26
Hope	Titus 2:13
Horn of Salvation	Luke 1:69
I Am	Exodus 3:14; John 8:58
Image of God	2 Corinthians 4:4
Image of His Person	Hebrews 1:3 (KJV)
Immanuel	Isaiah 7:14
Jehovah	Psalm 83:18 (KJV)
Jesus	Matthew 1:21
Judge	Isaiah 33:22; Acts 10:42

King	Zechariah 9:9
King Eternal	1 Timothy 1:17
King of Kings	1 Timothy 6:15
King of the Ages	Revelation 15:3
Lamb of God	John 1:29
Last Adam	1 Corinthians 15:45
Lawgiver	Isaiah 33:22
Leader	Isaiah 55:4
Life	John 14:6
Light of the World	John 8:12
Like an Eagle	Deuteronomy 32:11
Lily of the Valley	Song of Solomon 2:1
Lion of the Tribe of Judah	Revelation 5:5
Living Stone	1 Peter 2:4
Living Water	John 4:10
Lord	John 13:13
Lord God Almighty	Revelation 15:3
Lord Jesus Christ	1 Corinthians 15:57
Lord of All	Acts 10:36
Lord of Glory	1 Corinthians 2:8
Lord of Lords	1 Timothy 6:15
Lord Our Righteousness	Jeremiah 23:6
Love	1 John 4:8
Man of Sorrows	Isaiah 53:3
Master	Luke 5:5
Mediator	1 Timothy 2:5
Merciful	Jeremiah 3:12
Messenger of the Covenant	Malachi 3:1
Messiah	John 4:25
Mighty God	Isaiah 9:6
Mighty One	Isaiah 60:16
Nazarene	Matthew 2:23

Offspring of David	Revelation 22:16
Omega	Revelation 22:13
Only Begotten Son	John 1:18 (KJV)
Our Passover Lamb	1 Corinthians 5:7
Our Peace	Ephesians 2:14
Potter	Isaiah 29:16
Power of God	1 Corinthians 1:24
Prince of Peace	Isaiah 9:6
Prophet	Acts 3:22
Purifier	Malachi 3:3
Rabboni (Teacher)	John 20:16
Radiance of God's Glory	Hebrews 1:3
Redeemer	Job 19:25
Refiner's Fire	Malachi 3:2
Resurrection and the Life	John 11:25
Righteous One	1 John 2:1
Rock	1 Corinthians 10:4
Root of David	Revelation 22:16
Rose of Sharon	Song of Solomon 2:1
Ruler of God's Creation	Revelation 3:14
Ruler of the Kings of the Earth	Revelation 1:5
Ruler Over Israel	Micah 5:2
Savior	Luke 2:11
Scepter out of Israel	Numbers 24:17
Seed	Genesis 3:15
Servant	Isaiah 42:1
Shepherd and Overseer of Your Souls	1 Peter 2:25
Shield	Genesis 15:1
Son of David	Matthew 1:1
Son of God	Matthew 27:54
Son of Man	Matthew 8:20

Son of the Most High	Luke 1:32
Source of Eternal Salvation	Hebrews 5:9
Spirit of God	Genesis 1:2
Star out of Jacob	Numbers 24:17
Stone	1 Peter 2:8
Sun of Righteousness	Malachi 4:2
Teacher	John 13:13
True Light	John 1:9
True Witness	Revelation 3:14
Truth	John 14:6
Vine	John 15:5
Way	John 14:6
Wisdom of God	1 Corinthians 1:24
Witness	Isaiah 55:4
Wonderful Counselor	Isaiah 9:6
Word	John 1:1
Word of God	Revelation 19:13

NOTES

1. Taken from "May the Mind of Christ My Savior" and used by permission of the executors of the estate of the Reverend A. C. Barham Gould.
2. Taken from the hymn "We Come, O Christ, to Thee" by E. Margaret Clarkson. © by InterVarsity Christian Fellowship of the USA and used by permission of InterVarsity Press, Downers Grove, IL 60515.
3. THE SILVER CHAIR by C.S. Lewis copyright © C.S. Lewis Pte. Ltd. 1950. Extract reprinted by permission.
4. THE LION, THE WITCH AND THE WARDROBE by C.S. Lewis copyright © C.S. Lewis Pte. Ltd. 1950. Extract reprinted by permission.
5. Robert B. Girdlestone, *Synonyms of the Old Testament*, reprint ed. (Grand Rapids: Eerdmans, 1974), 32–34.
6. Ibid., 95–98.
7. THE LAST BATTLE by C.S. Lewis copyright © C.S. Lewis Pte. Ltd. 1950. Extract reprinted by permission.

ABOUT
THE AUTHOR

*M*ary Foxwell Loeks grew up in Japan, the daughter of missionary parents. After graduation from Wheaton College she taught at the elementary and pre-school levels for eleven years. Mary and her husband, John, live in Grand Rapids, Michigan, where for twenty years she served as Minister of Education at Church of the Servant. She has three married children and five grandchildren.